T0169517

THE CIRCLE OF *Fire*

Readers' Praise for
THE CIRCLE OF *Fire*

I felt myself being filled with gratitude and hope as I moved through the pages of the book. Yes, I cried, but I also laughed out loud. I felt a renewed spirit of strength and endurance to run my own race and fulfill my unique purpose.

—**Beverly Dracos**, President of Dracos Genuine Communications, LLC, writer, speaker, consultant, Co-author of *The Relationship Age*, with Mari Smith and Nick Nanton

Justina, this book is a masterpiece. You are as dynamic a writer as you are a speaker and person. Your passionate spirit witnesses so beautifully to your faith and shares it like sunshine. All can derive strength and direction from reading and reacting to this book. Flashbacks to the past, as related to the story, add dimension and transition. Thank you for sharing this book with me.

—**Gail Miller**, artist and writer

I would definitely recommend this book, but my recommendation would not be limited just to burn survivors and caregivers. Although the challenges in the book may be dealing with the devastation of burn injury and trauma, the process of recovery is universal and the realizations shared in Justina's journey from victim to survivor can be applicable to anyone who picks up this book.

—**Dennis Gardin**, Executive Director of the Georgia Firefighter Burn Foundation

The emotional connection I felt to this book centered on the author's explanation of what was happening to her inwardly. I was drawn in from a personal level and included on the path to healing and deliverance.

—**Lori Smith**, Houston, TX

I strongly recommend this book because it is good to know that someone out there can relate to how you feel while going through tragedy or loss. It is somewhat comforting to know that you aren't alone in how you feel. It is an eye-opener for caretakers, revealing how deeply the person in the tragedy could be affected.

—**Julia Francis**, Sugarland, TX

Reading this book brought back feelings—feelings I didn't even know I had. Everyone thought I was mad. I was trying to figure life out. What had I done wrong? Yes, this book put my feelings into words, very deep personal feelings that are hard to tell people.

—**Captain Darin Unruh**, Houston Fire Department, burn survivor

THE CIRCLE OF *Fire*

*In the Midst of the Ashes
an Ember of Hope Flickered*

JUSTINA PAGE

New York

THE CIRCLE OF *Fire*

In the Midst of the Ashes an Ember of Hope Flickered

© 2016 JUSTINA PAGE.

All rights reserved. No portion of this book may be reproduced, stored in a retrieval system, or transmitted in any form or by any means—electronic, mechanical, photocopy, recording, scanning, or other—except for brief quotations in critical reviews or articles, without the prior written permission of the publisher.

Published in New York, New York, by Morgan James Publishing. Morgan James and The Entrepreneurial Publisher are trademarks of Morgan James, LLC.
www.MorganJamesPublishing.com

The Morgan James Speakers Group can bring authors to your live event. For more information or to book an event visit The Morgan James Speakers Group at www.TheMorganJamesSpeakersGroup.com.

The Amos House of Faith
www.theamoshouse.org

All Scripture is taken from the King James Version of the Holy Bible.

A **free** eBook edition is available
with the purchase of this print book.

CLEARLY PRINT YOUR NAME ABOVE IN UPPER CASE

Instructions to claim your free eBook edition:
1. Download the BitLit app for Android or iOS
2. Write your name in **UPPER CASE** on the line
3. Use the BitLit app to submit a photo
4. Download your eBook to any device

ISBN 978-1-63047-208-5 paperback
ISBN 978-1-63047-209-2 eBook
Library of Congress Control Number:
2014935915

Editor:
Gail Miller

Photo Credit:
Norma Goulette

Cover Design by:
Rachel Lopez
www.r2cdesign.com

Interior Design by:
Bonnie Bushman
The Whole Caboodle Graphic Design

In an effort to support local communities and raise awareness and funds, Morgan James Publishing donates a percentage of all book sales for the life of each book to Habitat for Humanity Peninsula and Greater Williamsburg.

Get involved today, visit
www.MorganJamesBuilds.com

DEDICATION

*This book is dedicated in memory of my precious twin son Amos Beniah Page
and in memory of my spiritual mother Sister Norma J. Jones.
God has taken them back to himself.
They have finished their race and now rest safely on heaven's shores.*

TABLE OF CONTENTS

FOREWORD

Tragedy, hope, love, and sorrow are all part of the fabric of life, the exact design of which we, as individuals, often have no choice in. When there is a tragedy, we can only feel a sense of insufferable loss. Such is life.

Justina Page and her family's lives were changed forever on the morning of March 7, 1999, when her home was engulfed in flames. Her home was destroyed, and she and her husband lost their twenty-two-month-old twin son Amos. The other twin was severely injured; Justina Page survived but was left with third-degree burns over 50 percent of her body.

The Circle of Fire is a must-read for those who have faced trials and tribulations or have come to the crossroads of life wanting to give up. Life doesn't offer mankind the option of knowing what we may face in the future, but we should be encouraged to persevere. Regardless of how bad the situation gets, there's always hope.

—**Chief Rick Flanagan**, Executive Assistant Fire Chief
of the Houston Fire Department

ACKNOWLEDGMENT

I would like to acknowledge, first and foremost, my Lord and Savior, Jesus Christ, in whom I live and move and have my being (Acts 17:28). Who, despite the unexpected turns that life tends to take, has given me the strength to endure life's most ferocious storms and thrive with my dignity and integrity intact. My life has not been the same since I was adopted into the royal family. To my husband, friend, and soul mate, James R. Page Jr., thank you so much for your unconditional love, respect, and strength. You hold me close enough to keep me from danger while also giving me freedom to chase a dream. Your commitment to the boys and me has earned you the right to wear the purple heart of valor that should grace the neck of many unsung heroes. To my sons, Jonathon, Joseph, Caleb, Daniel, Amos, and Benjamin, God knew what he was doing when he filled my quiver with six baby boys. I love you all, and I am trusting that God will bring you all to the fulfillment of his will for your lives.

To the Full Gospel Church of Love In Christ, thank you for loving me in deed and in truth. I appreciate every dinner prepared, every therapy trip made, every visit, every prayer, and every tear shed. This book would not be possible without the example you set. To my many family members and friends who supported us financially, spiritually, and otherwise, thank you. I pray your reward is great.

To the staff on the John S. Dunn Sr. Burn Unit at Memorial Hermann Hospital in Houston, Texas, keep up the good work. The care you provide is exemplary. To Dr. Donald Parks, my surgeon and friend, thanks for your exceptional medical skills and impeccable bedside manner. Your support of our mission is greatly appreciated. To Dr. Richard Wainerdi, the Texas Medical Center President, thanks for your continual support and keen ability to understand and move with a vision.

To my peer review team, thank you. Your honesty and insightful feedback smoothed out the rough edges of the manuscript, allowing me to proclaim my message in a powerful way. To my writing coach, Jan King, thanks for believing in me. Your enthusiasm and expertise has brought this book to life. To my marketing team, Beverly Dracos and Ellen O'Connor, thanks for your endless hours of work and dedication to this project. I appreciate your authentic belief in the power of the message contained in this book—a message designed to empower and change the lives of those who are hurting and need understanding on how to travel the challenging terrain of tragedy.

SPECIAL ACKNOWLEDGMENT

Thank you for your ongoing support of The Amos House of Faith.
Many burn survivors will be comforted
because of you!

Common Voices
www.fireadvocates.org

Dracos Genuine Communications, LLC
www.genuinecommunications.com

Ellen O'Connor
Remote Assistance and Design
www.radladies.com

Minger Family
www.mingerfoundation.org

National Fire Sprinkler Association, PenJerDel Chapter
http://www.nfsa.org

The Amos House of Faith
www.theamoshouse.org

INTRODUCTION

We were your typical Christian family: a husband, his wife, and six sons. Living a blessed and happy life, we were believers who attended services, volunteered in the community, and enjoyed family outings. Then it happened: a four-alarm house fire. It was the life-altering tragedy that rocked our whole world.

Why God? Where were you? What did we do? I had so many unanswered questions. The answers were a long time in coming. But they eventually came.

The statistics regarding burn injuries in the United States are staggering. There are over two million burn injuries reported each year. Burn injuries are in the top five most common reasons of accidental death. Fires kill over five hundred children under the age of fourteen each year, making them the leading cause of accidental death for children. Burns are the most expensive accidental injuries to treat. Sadly, fires and burns are more commonplace than people may realize; they kill more people every year than any other force of nature.

While deadly, fire is inordinately helpful for everyday duties. It is a chemical reaction between oxygen in the atmosphere and some sort of fuel, a combustion reaction that happens when you heat the fuel to its ignition temperature. A fire will continue to burn as long as there is fuel and oxygen around it. When it makes contact with flesh, the result is a burn. Though less apparent, there is also an internal fire set when one experiences a burn trauma. There is an emotional reaction between the faith in your heart and the fuel of fear and anger. The result is devastation and confusion.

This book deals with the hard questions burn victims, or indeed anyone suffering an event beyond his control, may ask: Why? How? What next? That last question, for me, was the most crucial. For a long time, I didn't have an answer. It was a long while before I could make sense of the event or make peace with the loss. This text is an account of our family's tumultuous journey through the trauma and pain fire can bring. I share how we learned that devastation and catastrophe are not a life sentence to despair. Instead, hard times can be a stepping stone to purpose and vision.

There are many types of fires in this life: emotional, relational, financial, and otherwise. We may not be able to prevent hardships, but we can prepare for the inevitable dark days that will come.

I am sharing my account of my family's journey from burn victims to burn survivors for several reasons. First, I have heard many well-meaning friends and loved ones attempt to communicate my experience and feelings, and they have fallen painfully short of the reality. Their intent was not malicious; it's just that no one can really pinpoint your exact feelings but you. For a long time, my voice has been silent, allowing others to draw conclusions as it suited them. I feel it is time to set the record straight.

Secondly, what we have been through collectively as a family, and also as seven individuals, is not an isolated experience. Tragedies happen every day. There have been many before us, and unfortunately, there will be more to follow. Those who are yet to experience loss can benefit from the wisdom that hindsight affords us. There is a healing process that is initiated when emotions and truth are released. Through writing, I discovered the depths of my own feelings as they were revealed and exposed on the written page.

Finally and most importantly, I want to help validate the mixed assortment of conflicting feelings shared by burn survivors—feelings that are not so easily understood and are often misconstrued.

My wish is that by the end of this journey, others will be revitalized, encouraged, and full of faith in the purposes that God has set for their lives. I pray that, in full assurance of faith, they will enjoy sunshine while it is present and endure the storms that catch us off guard.

James & Justina Page —wedding day May 30, 1987

Chapter 1

INFERNO

Oh my God! The house is on fire!

At the crack of dawn on March 7, 1999, something goes terribly wrong. I awake to explosions, smoke, and darkness. Oh, my God! The house is on fire.

Our family is jolted from our peaceful bliss and thrown into chaos in a home totally engulfed with flames. The sound of appliances exploding is deafening. The heat and stench throw us into confusion and shock.

My husband, James, begins frantically jumping in and out of windows, desperate to save me and our young children. The three oldest boys grab their younger autistic brother and wait at a pre-designated point for their father.

I am the first to be dropped from a window, but I am hysterical. I reenter the inferno, determined to reach my twenty-two-month-old twin boys. I am pinned

1

by a large, burning, oak bookshelf that falls on me. I am trapped, burning, and unable to speak above a whisper. My husband sees me under the bookshelf and shoves me out our bedroom window again.

I crawl from the window to the front lawn, leaving pieces of burned flesh as I go. My hands are so badly injured that I can no longer use them to support myself. I shout from the edge of the street where a neighbor is steadying me by pressing her head to mine.

"I have six sons! Get my babies!"

But the count of sons who made it out never reaches six.

The house collapses before my husband is able to get our son Amos out. He dies in the fire.

Amos's twin, Benjamin, and I are severely injured.

I drift in and out of oblivion. The paramedics try their best to rouse me. "Breathe," one of them says. "Please breathe, baby!"

Tears are falling down his face. *That can't be good*, I think. I hear panic in his voice.

Then I hear another voice, an unearthly voice, the cry of a fearful, wild animal. But it is Benjamin's voice.

I cannot bear the thought of Benjamin feeling the horrific pain I am experiencing.

I pass out, succumbing to utter darkness.

What a difference a day can make. The day before, I woke up bright and early, even before the twins were stirring. Our church was having a Saturday morning breakfast, and the teenagers were our appointed chefs. I was one of the chaperones for the event. I snatched up the seven, blue, "Heaven Scent" aprons I had made to surprise the girls, kissed my husband good-bye, and scurried out with "see you later" hanging between us.

By the time the church members arrived, the church was filled with an assortment of enticing aromas: crisp bacon, juicy sausage, crunchy hash browns, fluffy pancakes, and every fruit and juice you can imagine. The fellowship was as refreshing as the food. I was a true busy bee that day.

My husband oversaw the boys for me. I particularly remember him holding Amos for the greater portion of the day. I thought it odd but never got around to asking him why. The day ended with me taking a trip to the mall with my pastor's wife and two other ladies. The last thing I remember her saying to me when I got out of the car was, "I love you."

I staggered into the house and sat on the first seat I saw. It was our green Queen Anne wingback chair, which I had every intention of reupholstering but never got around to doing. I was exhausted. I let everything drop to the ground.

James came to the front room and smiled a mischievous smile. "Tired, dear?" he asked, teasing me. I rolled my eyes. He kissed me on the forehead and laughed.

"I put the kids down for you. Your work is over for tonight."

The relief was instantaneous. Thank God for my husband. My custom was to iron seven pants, seven shirts, and one dress the night before church. I managed a grateful thank you to my husband and told him I would iron in the morning. By some act of divine intervention, I got dressed for bed. I was beyond tired.

When I knelt on my knees to pray, I remember praying the shortest and strangest prayer in my life: "Lord, have mercy." Those three words were all I could manage to say. With that, I snuggled next to my husband and welcomed slumber, anticipating another great Sunday morning.

Early that Sunday morning, however, my husband found himself at the Memorial Hermann Hospital Burn Unit with two elder sons in shock and two other sons with serious first-and second-degree burns. His wife and toddler son were in surgery, fighting for their lives, and he was missing a twin baby boy, the son he had held in his arms so tenderly just hours before. Catastrophe had hit the Page family head-on. We had suffered a vicious impact, and we never saw it coming. In the blink of an eye, life as we knew it was no more. There was no more home, no clothes, food, toys, books, or pictures. The most painful reality could hardly be absorbed: there was no more Amos. Our family had stepped into a new, chaotic existence where stability had vanished.

I had never in my life experienced tragedy on this level. The closest I had ever come to misfortune was an event during my seventh grade year of junior high school. I was on the Southeast Community Center tumbling team, the Aero Dynamics. I loved that group. We wore gray and powder blue warm up suits with shiny, silver lettering. I felt so honored to be on the team. When we did tumbling routines, the silver would look magical, like streaks of lightning flashing. We had an opportunity to do a halftime performance for the Kansas City Kings basketball team at Kemper Arena.

My excitement was over the top. I can still feel the thrill of hearing the announcer introduce us: "And now, for your halftime entertainment, the Aero Dynamics." The crowd went ballistic. The cheers and roars were deafening. It was an adrenaline rush like none other. Every performance ended with the top seven tumblers showcasing their skills. I was not the number one performer, but I was in that elite group. It was my turn to shine. When performing, you are taught not to stray too far from your experience and training. I was doing a series of backflips, getting faster and more confident as I went. The crowd was egging me on. The shouts and the cheers and my pride persuaded me to ignore the inner bell that told me I was way past my normal limit.

The momentum was building, and I was not letting go of the moment. That is, until my arms gave out on me, and I fell to the floor with a loud thud. A collective gasp sounded from the crowd. Then complete silence filled the arena, followed by my shrill cry from the pain. I had dislocated my elbow and broken my arm in several places. The crowd graciously applauded me as the stretcher took me away. My pride was seriously wounded. I went to school and never bothered to share with anyone the reason I had a cast on

Top: Grandpa & Grandma Page comforting Joseph at funeral
Left: Daddy at funeral holding Daniel's hand

my arm. For a middle school student, dislocating an elbow and breaking an arm in the middle of Kemper Arena was a top-notch tragedy, particularly for an independent child like myself. I had to depend on others to carry my book bag, a major offense. My little heart traversed through many of the same stages I would revisit as an adult: loss of control, fear, loss, anger, pain, and guilt. However, this small mishap in no way prepared me for the devastation to come.

I never really talked to anyone who could give me advice; there were no volunteers on the floor, just doctors and nurses. I walked the halls to see and talk to other burn patients to see how well off I was. Time is a good healer, and after you get out of the hospital, the real work begins. It's time for rehab. I just knew I had to cope and adapt to what was to come. You must get your head to acknowledge what has happened and get your heart into it and accept it—then things really start to fall into place.

—**Gary Alley**, burn survivor and Amos House of Faith volunteer

After the fire, many of our out-of-state friends and relatives came to support us. Unfortunately, I was in a coma too long to acknowledge their presence. It was still comforting to know they came. That they cared enough to pack up and come several states away and make themselves available to help meant so much. King Solomon encouraged us in the book of Ecclesiastes to "cast thy bread upon the waters" (11:1). It is a good rule to live by. If you touch someone's life with kindness, that kindness will reach back and touch you. Life is uncertain. We never know what a day may bring. In the day that tragedy takes over, you never know who will be there to help.

As a stay-at-home mom with six sons, I had no choice but to be creative in guiding my household. I would create games like "Where's the Toys?" to keep toys off the floor and out of my kitchen after playtime. We would play "Who Remembered?" to make sure baths were done properly.

My twins had come as a complete surprise. I had a midwife with that pregnancy and was so confident that I was going to have a girl that I did not want an ultrasound. I figured, who would have another boy after having four boys in a row? Two weeks prior to my delivery, the babies changed positions and disclosed themselves. I did go ahead and get that ultrasound, secretly thanking God for giving me twin girls. You know the end of the story.

After the twins were born, I came up with an ingenious game called "That's My Baby." I had assigned my two oldest sons, Jonathon and Joseph, a twin each. They each wanted to make sure that his baby was safe, his bottle was clean, his blanket or toy provided. For a mother of six, this game was fun.

Jonathon's baby was Amos, and Joseph's baby was Benjamin. They took this responsibility seriously. The fire showed this game to be detrimental. Jonathon had to be held down by three adults to keep him from rushing toward the burning house to get Amos. The door exploded thirty seconds after they tackled him. He was determined to make sure his baby was safe.

Because of the emotional load I was pulling following the fire, I never considered the trauma Jonathon was dealing with. I regret that omission to this day. The fact that he didn't bear the outward burn scars, like Benjamin and me, deceived me. Our entire family shared almost all of the inward wounds: faith crisis, anger, survivor's guilt, loss, and so forth. But Jonathon had also lost *his* baby. In his nine-year-old mind, he had failed in his responsibility. I never acknowledged his pain and regret. The bad choices and the rebellion that followed were the repercussions. My children were the silent sufferers.

Jonathon celebrating at Dad's birthday

I lost everything that was mine
—Jonathon Page

About four years after the fire, the boys and I were sitting in the living room, doing various activities and enjoying each other's company. Out of the blue, Joseph blurted out, "I am a coward." I was astonished. "What did you say?" I asked.

He held his head down low as he removed his glasses and rubbed the bridge of his nose. Then he said something that pains me to this day.

"Remember the fire? I only saved myself."

Remember the fire? In that moment, I saw my mistake. He had not been adequately included in this crisis. Physically, he had suffered the least and felt the guilt of that distinction.

For the first time, I realized clearly that this was not my crisis alone. This was a family crisis. My children had problems. My husband had problems. Everybody was suffering. Joseph had done exactly what he or any other eight-year-old was supposed to do, yet he had apparently spent four years tormented by inappropriate feelings.

> *I am a coward. Remember the fire? I only saved myself.*
> **—Joseph Page**

Before the fire, I had homeschooled my sons, an important privilege in my eyes. After the fire, grief made homeschooling difficult, so I chose to enroll the boys in public school a year after I was released from the hospital. I tried my best to be there for my kids. I became the PTO president for the elementary school and the PTO secretary at the middle school. Most of the kids knew me, spoke to me, and treated me with respect.

Joseph celebrating at Dad's birthday party

As was my custom, one day after school, I asked Caleb about his day. This day I did not see that enormous grin I had become accustomed to seeing. He was silent. His gaze was pointed, and I knew he had something serious to say.

"Can I tell you something, Mom, something that you don't know?" he said slowly.

"Sure." I had no know idea what to expect.

"The kids are nice when you are around, but when you leave, they talk about you and tease me. I hate school." He held back the tears that were threatening to expose themselves.

You could have bought me for a penny. I was lost for words. I had no idea that elementary children were that skilled in the art of deception.

The kids are nice when you are around, but when
you leave, they talk about you and tease me.
—Caleb Page

Caleb celebrating at
Dad's birthday party

Chapter 2

SUNSHINE

"Lord," I said within my heart, "if something terrible
were ever to happen, would I be able to remain faithful?"

M y husband and I had the fortunate experience to fall in love for the first time with each other. Our first apartment was in an off-campus apartment complex called the A Frames. It was a studio apartment that had windows from the floor to the ceiling, shaped in an actual A. On the top level was our desk for studying; the middle floor was our bedroom; and the bottom level held the living room, dining room, bathroom, and kitchen. The sunshine would often wake me before the alarm. I would lie in his arms, thinking how blessed I was to have this wonderful man as my husband.

Two years after we were married, our family began to grow. The first touch that each son felt at birth was the hands of his father. Life in a household of males, my six little princes and King James, as I affectionately called them, was very entertaining. We were a busy lot. My whole world seemed to revolve around field trips, lunch dates with Dad, vacations, and birthday parties.

One of our favorite sunshiny moments was the time my husband had to travel to Washington, DC, to install a unit for a customer of his company. The timeframe for the completion of the job was six weeks. Since I was a homeschool mom, the boys and I joined him and made an extended vacation out of it. Every morning when my husband set off for work, we would pack lunches, load up the double stroller, and set off for an adventure. We would visit parks, museums, the zoo, and monuments. The sun was bright, the cool breeze comforting, and each moment perfect. Life for our family, in general, was full of laughter, fun, and contentment.

In February of 1999, I had been happily married for eleven years. We were only three months shy of our twelfth wedding anniversary. The fruit of the union was six beautiful baby boys: four single births and one set of twins. My husband was a senior electrical engineer for High Tech, a Holland-based engineering firm. I was a Sunday school teacher and homeschool mom who ran a science lab for Houston homeschoolers. Life was good, peaceful, fulfilling; life was perfect. And then, I asked God a question.

"Lord", I said within my heart, "since I have given my life to you, nothing terrible has ever happened to me. If something terrible were ever to happen, would I be able to remain faithful?" Some questions are rhetorical, but I didn't know the honest answer. More importantly, I really wanted to know what kind of stuff I was made of in the deep recesses of my heart. I suppose a simple yes or no would not have satisfied me. My personality type demanded that I be shown.

My deepest fears were often put under subjection through denial. I had an innate defense mechanism that shielded me from the terror of my misfortune. Faith was the instrument that

Page boys

allowed me to live peacefully, despite the myriad of tragedies happening all around me. Without faith, fear would have had dominion over my peace. It is easy to accept the reality of tragedies when you assume it will not happen to you.

King Solomon said in the book of Ecclesiastes, "The race is not to the swift, nor the battle to the strong, neither yet bread to the wise, nor yet riches to men of understanding, nor yet favor to men of skill; but time and chance happeneth to them all" (9:11). The operative word here is *chance*. Chance is scary because there are no indicators to track it. The great challenge is avoiding fear while acknowledging chance.

Acknowledging chance while refusing to be shaken by uncertainty is a delicate balance. It is the happy medium between optimism and pessimism. My good friend Lori and I often had discussions about our "what ifs." We would ask each other, "What would you think or do *if* this or that were to happen?"

One day during our theoretical discussions, Sister Lori posed the following question: "If you heard a fire truck in the distance, would your first instinct be that it is coming to your house or to the neighbor's?"

I shocked her and myself. My answer was instantaneous: my house. My response did not seem to fit my personality. I had faith to believe the sun could be made to stand still. Somehow, though, I instinctively understood something about chance. While I never sat around in fear of something happening to me, I just couldn't rule it out. The question I couldn't answer was this: if the fire truck is coming, why would it be the neighbor's house instead of mine?

We believe that the fire originated in the attic and was due to faulty wiring. It didn't even occur to me until well after the incident that this tragedy had a point of origin. It was a while into the tragedy before I even thought to inquire about the details. The fire marshal's report came back stating the cause as "undetermined." That was irritating. *Undetermined* sounded so callous, a lot like, "Who cares?" A fire had taken the life of my son, obliterated every possession we owned, and changed our family forever, yet no one could identify the source. There was an evil enemy out there that I could not pinpoint. There was no one or nothing to blame or take responsibility for such a great loss.

Something evil happened in our attic.
–Joseph Page

It is amazing the enormous impact that one event can have in your life. The fire was such a monumental moment for us that it became a point of reference to mark family events. The majority of our family's memorable moments are divided and referred to as a pre-fire or post-fire event. When we are together, trying to recall an occasion, the first question asked is, "Was that before or after the fire?"

The fire altered the way I perceive life. I had always felt that bad things didn't happen to good people. It's odd now that I think about it. In thinking that nothing would happen to me, I was insinuating that I was good. That's pretty bold. I felt that I was a child of God and that his divine protection would not allow any bad thing—much less any horrific thing—to happen to me. I felt if I did good things and treated people right, like God instructed, then only good things would happen to me. So when something bad happened, I was momentarily stumped. What an intriguing path of discovery I had to travel.

There is this thing called "life that just happens." It has an assortment of experiences in its bag. Just like a bag of Brach's assorted candies, some experiences are to our liking and others make us sour in the face. The challenge is to live through it all. We cannot separate the good times from the bad times, nor can we choose which good time or bad time we will experience. The bag of life is designed in such a way that you experience it all—or not.

The movement of fire is set on course by the path of the fuel igniting it. As it travels, it rises to a destructive fury. The emotional trial and fire that burns within a burn survivor follows a similar path, beginning and ending at the person you are within. Trauma is a terribly inconvenient method of bringing the real you to the forefront. Yet it can become one of the most amazing discoveries in your life. We are all dealt a hand in this life, from birth. No matter what that hand is, when we reach the age of accountability, it is up to us to play it well and win.

In the popular movie *The Lion King*, the lyrics in the song "The Circle of Life" reflect the typical burn survivor's journey: "Some of us sail through our troubles, and some have to live with the scars." After a burn trauma, some people do fall by the wayside, yet some soar to the stars. The circle of fire forces burn survivors to move forward through fear, loss, anger, pain, despair, and guilt—until we find ourselves triumphant, hopeful, purposeful, and comfortable in our own skin again. Every experience is unique, yet those who suffer share so much in common. I want to encourage all burn survivors to keep pushing forward. With the proper help and encouragement, no one has to fall by the wayside; everyone has an opportunity to soar.

Everyone enjoys sunshine. Sunshine incites your expectations. The brilliance of its bright rays feels like the down payment of promises to come. We love to bask in the radiant cheerfulness that sunshine brings; it's a good, fuzzy feeling deep inside that covers us.

Yet not every day is graced with sunshine. There are days when the clouds take charge; days when the bullies come out; days when wind, rain, and lightning mingle and intertwine themselves in the form of a storm, threatening our peace and safety. The feelings of uncertainty take advantage of us. When will the storm stop? Where is the sun? We search for cover, consolation, or protection—anything to help us wait out the frightful storm.

After a while, the howling of the wind and the thrashing of the rain cannot be heard. You timidly peek from your hiding place and discover that the sunshine has returned. This time it seems even more brilliant. It is the same sun, really, but you are more grateful for it. So it is with those whose lives have been interrupted by the storms that burn trauma brings on. I have been there. I have waited and wondered, *Is there an end? Will the sun shine in my life again?*

Take it from me. It is possible to see sunny days again. I have learned that storms don't last always. Nature itself confirms my discovery. Every day, the sun rises, and every day, it goes down at God's command.

Anything can happen to any of us at any time, simply because we live on the planet earth. Our character, be it good or bad, does not determine our exposure to trouble. Neither does it necessarily follow that every human will experience tragedy.

Take consolation that the experience of tragedy doesn't set you in a special group of people called "bad." Bad things *do* happen to good people—just like good things happen to bad people. The wisdom I have learned from my tragic experience is this: things just happen. Where the rubber meets the road is in realizing that no matter what happens, we have to deal with it. It's how we choose to deal with those things that occur in our life that is of consequential importance.

Chapter 3

CRISIS

Our needs were enormous

T he time span between passing out in the ambulance and waking up on a ventilator seemed to be a few moments. However, I was actually in a medically induced coma for right under two months. I remember two distinct experiences. The first was a terrifying nightmare where I was on a pole, like a rotisserie chicken, being cooked slowly while people looked on from the stands. The other was the voice of a friend weeping over me, saying she had no idea that she loved me so much. Otherwise, I simply slept, unaware of the magnitude of the turmoil my husband was dealing with.

A moment in time had transitioned him from being a proud father of six to being the caretaker of two severely burned family members and four traumatized young sons—all while grieving the loss of his child. Like always, he was responsible for clothing, sheltering, and providing. But now, his days were even more hectic and tiring. Days began early, with dropping the kids off to the babysitter and school. After a full day of work, he would visit Benjamin and me and get updates from Dr. Parks. Afterward, he would pick up the kids and feed them, bathe them, and prepare them for the next day.

Our needs were enormous. Thankfully, the Houston community came to our aid in a big way. They graciously donated an abundance of food, money, furniture, clothes, and toys. Our church family was a rock for us as well. They set up prayer vigils and assisted with various daily tasks.

A crisis is an unstable and crucial time. When you are in a crisis, everyone and everything connected to you is affected on some level. The same fire created multiple crises for all of us. However, crises are not universal. Events affect people in different ways. What was a crisis for my children may not have been a crisis for me and vice versa. That is why it is difficult sometimes to discern when others are in a crisis.

One of the most devastating things about a crisis is that the answers elude us, yet they are the link to solid ground. When you face a crisis, you feel like you are sinking, all alone. It is hard to recognize those who are in the quicksand with you, even just a few inches away. I had been traumatized on multiple levels. My body was burned; I could not breathe on my own. One twin was dead, another twin burned, and all my children were hurt in some fashion. I had no home, no possessions, and the list of losses went on and on. I was so caught up in my personal anguish that I did not perceive the trauma that my three oldest sons were dealing with. I was consumed with the loss of my son, but I was not mindful that the boys had lost a brother—a perfectly healthy baby brother at that.

The ramifications for my sons were just as serious as they were for me. My children had been catapulted to a position against their will and left to deal with some heavy adult dilemmas, but with a child's mind. The combination of death, disfigurement, and loss can drive your average adult insane. How much worse it must be for children, whose greatest dilemma previously was which toy they would play with first.

Several well-meaning friends went on and on about how I must feel having huge keloids on the side of my neck and losing all the gifts my husband had just brought me from his business trip to Europe. The word "keloid" didn't mean anything to me at that time—I later discovered it meant abnormal scars—and I couldn't have told you what he had brought from Europe anyway. Those issues were minor compared to the real deal.

The real deal was my children. The real crisis was the death of my child and our physical and emotional recovery. I finally had to let my friends know, politely, that their comments weren't appropriate. What are scars and a gift compared to death and health?

When I was lying in the hospital bed in pain, discouraged and fearful, nothing was more encouraging than the visitor who said, "This is a good team of nurses and doctors," or "Wow, they are taking good care of you," or "The boys went to Chuck E Cheese today. They are so happy." Those comments helped me cope with the dilemma before me.

There are several things that I find helpful when trying to help someone in a crisis stage. First and foremost, you should make a great effort to get a good understanding of what is going on. What is the real problem? Clarification is essential. What is truly affecting them? It is not about you. When people you love and care for are in a crisis mode, you will likely have a crisis response yourself. However, one of the worst things you can do is to assume they feel the way you do.

My experience as a patient, caregiver, volunteer, and peer supporter has shown that the emotion or problem you had prior to the trauma is amplified afterward. Those who had anger management problems prior to their injury were time bombs afterward. Those who had self-esteem issues prior to injury tended to have a no confidence at all after. When circumstances overwhelm, victims may even go into shock and attempt to protect themselves through denial or detachment. These are normal emotional reactions to crisis.

Another common result of crisis is depression. Depression causes you to lose interest in the world around you. It's a state of hopelessness in which you feel that there's no use to carry on. My church family quickly pulled me out of that phase. They had a way of making me feel that my recovery was necessary for their happiness. Some of them checked on my therapy, nutrition, and medications. The congregation showed both love and wisdom in their care for me.

One of the most difficult phases of the crisis stage for me was the flashbacks. They were so vivid and real that it was torturous. My flashbacks usually occurred at night when I was most frightened. Just as I was about to give in to a peaceful slumber, I would hear Benjamin's unearthly voice, recall not being able to breathe, and relive the pain. Then I would jolt back to reality, sweaty, eyes wide, and robbed of peace.

Sometimes I would be rewrapping the bandages on my hands, and I would see myself at the edge of the lawn, the neighbor holding my head up with hers. I would see my flesh falling to the ground, as I cried out, tormented, for a count of my children—which never reached six. I found release from these flashbacks after I confided in a few friends, and we prayed them away. I never was bothered by these devastating visions again.

Triggers are circumstances or events that force you to relive the trauma experience, rekindling the same emotional experiences. It is not always easy to identify your triggers. The resulting emotions may last a little while, or they may be indefinite. Whatever the length, it is good to know what your triggers are. The first time I heard a siren in the hospital, I was petrified. I was bedridden and on a ventilator and couldn't go anywhere, but in my mind, I was running for my life. Our fire was a four-alarm fire. The sound of the siren took me right back to the edge of the lawn. The noise still has an effect on me but in a different way. Now when I hear a siren, I move quickly out of the way and encourage others to do the same. If I hear the siren at home, I pray for the lives in the ambulance.

One day about three years after the fire, I had promised James I would relax. The kids were at school, so I decided to do something I rarely did, eat popcorn and watch a movie alone. I had my legs propped on the living room table, enjoying my lighthearted comedy. Then a fire scene came on. A mother was at the edge of the street crying out for her child. I lost it.

Before I knew it, I was on the floor, weeping, praying that she would find her child. That scene was too close to home for me. I imagine that type of scene will always be a trigger for me.

Crises are personal. Whatever reaction you have to your personal trauma is nothing more than a normal reaction to an abnormal circumstance you have experienced. Crises are sudden and quick. Like a snake coiling to launch an attack, crises lie in wait, undisclosed, waiting for the optimum time to attack. The venom is lethal if help is not administered. Talking about it is freeing, promotes healing, and counteracts the poison of bitterness and fear.

A NOTE TO BURN SURVIVORS

A support system is invaluable. Those who have been in your shoes have a wealth of experience and compassion to offer. Be cautious not to become a hermit. A trusted friend could make the difference between life and death.

Prayer

Heavenly Father, I come to you in the name of Jesus.

I am on very shaky ground. What is happening to us?

I am afraid to pray and afraid not to pray.

I don't even know what to say.

If you don't help me, the stress will kill me before the burns do.

Why does my son have to go through this? Will we make it?

I have to trust in and lean on you.

The Lord is my shepherd: I shall not want. He maketh me to lie down in green pastures: he leadeth me beside the still waters. He restoreth my soul: he leadeth me in the paths of righteousness for his name's sake. Yea, though I walk through the valley of the shadow of death, I will fear no evil: for thou art with me; thy rod and thy staff they comfort me. Thou preparest a table before me in the presence of mine enemies: thou anointest my head with oil: my cup runneth over. Surely goodness and mercy shall follow me all the days of my life and I will dwell in the house of the Lord forever (Ps. 23).

Help quickly, please.

In Jesus' name,

Amen.

Chapter 4

LOSS OF CONTROL

I awake from a six-week coma, intubated,
disoriented, and in excruciating pain.

M y eyes slowly open, and they are as heavy as lead. I awake from a
six-week coma, intubated, disoriented, and in excruciating pain. It
is insanely hard to focus. What is that odd, overwhelming smell?
Why can't I breathe? What is this large obstruction down my throat? Suddenly, I
feel like I am losing my grasp on life; I feel the eerie nearness of death. I fight for
life. Why am I tied down? Where in the world am I? Where is my family—my
husband and my sons?

I plummet into a full-blown panic attack. The fire! Who lived? Who died?
Do I have a home? The pain is severe; it hurts to think. I want to talk, but I am
unable to. I have lost the ability to do anything on my own. I am dependent on

everyone for everything. My orderly world is out of control, and I am not in command of anything.

The ICU nurse must have notified my husband that I was awake. I hear footsteps approaching the door. I am unable to turn my head toward him, but I know it is him. I am very familiar with his presence.

I feel love and concern flowing from him before he even touches me. He is cautious and gentle. The depth of his love uplifts my spirit. We look into each other's eyes, determined to be strong. For a fleeting moment, everything is okay.

James begins to speak, but I cannot hear him. My thoughts and faith are battling each other. The strong façade is fading. I am tumbling, out of control again. He cannot see the sudden withdrawal of courage. The retreat all takes place inside. I know he would have saved me from this freefall if he had known it was happening, but the descent is concealed.

It was easy to predict who my next visitor would be. I would have been shocked to see anyone else but my pastor, Bishop A. Jones, and his loving wife, Norma J. Jones. They are the essence of love and faith. They enter the room with my husband and his cousin, Minister Richardson. I see determination on my pastor's face.

There is something they need to tell me. My senses instantly awaken. *What is it?* Anything could have happened while I was comatose. I know bad news is coming. My heart begins to beat in an irregular pattern. I feel like I am going to faint. I want to escape the news, whatever it is, but I am cornered. I silently pray, "Lord, please help; give me strength. I can't—"

My prayer is interrupted by my pastor's voice. I tune in fully; I am accustomed to listening intently when he speaks. He makes eye contact. There is no turning back.

My heart is breaking into a million pieces as he speaks. I want to scream, lash out, stomp, and break something—anything but just lie there. But, I can't move. I have to take the beating of the news like a slave tied to a whipping pole; the words are like lashes striking my spirit.

I am still intubated, so I cannot even vocalize my hurt and pain. All I can do is let the tears flow and nod to acknowledge that I have heard what he said.

There was a devastating fire.

We lost our home and everything we own.

Joseph and Jonathon were treated for smoke inhalation and released the next day.

Caleb and Daniel suffered first- and second-degree burns and were released the following week.

Benjamin suffered second- and third-degree burns on his face and upper extremities. He is in the pediatric unit and is also intubated. He has been in the hospital as long as I have.

When a family has to sustain so much change, the heart and soul can take as long to heal as the injury itself. When everything is out of your control, the strongest will feel the most helpless. We're so glad the worst is over.
–**Shameka Marshall**, ABC Club mom

And then he tells me.

Amos is gone.

My baby, my son, my precious child is no more.

I go numb. I am in shock. My heart had tried to notify me about Amos's death, but I ignored the signal. Hearing someone else vocalize it made it all too real.

The confirmation of his death rocked me. I felt myself entering a strange place. I saw a morbid image: my husband burying Benjamin and me. I imagined him going into a depression and the children being left all alone.

That last image jolted my motherly instincts. I would fight to the death for my children. I was sure of it. I had already proven my protective nature by running through fire to save them. They would not be left alone if I could help it. A lifeline had been thrown to me that I had not anticipated.

I had something to live for. I had five surviving children and a devoted husband. Yes, I had lost control, and yes, my world had been horribly disrupted, and yes, my health was hanging by a thread. Even so, I had something powerful left: I had a mind and a will. I couldn't move or talk, but I could desire to do so. I would fight.

Even though I could not summon my will at that moment, I would not starve my desire. I would do one more thing. I would pray. Angry, fearful, confused, and hurt, I would still pray. I would talk to the one I had trusted my soul to. Jesus was the only one I had ever talked to with my mouth closed and my voice silent anyway.

As an adult, finding out that you are not in control is difficult. You become childlike in that everything you want to get or do depends on the adults in charge. In the case of a burn unit, the grownups who supervise the pain, fear, and anger are doctors, nurses, and therapists. They control the how, when, and where each event occurs. And they can be merciless, though it's often for your own good.

When I was a child and we lived in Los Angeles, my mother ran a taco house and sold cool cups, which were frozen Kool-Aid drinks in a variety of flavors. The customers' favorite cool cup was fruity patootie, a mixture of all the flavors combined.

We made a commission on our sales, so we developed an entrepreneurial spirit early on. Every night, we would fill the freezer with cool cups in anticipation of making a profit the next day. Every night, my mother would also set a large can of peaches in the refrigerator next to the Kool-Aid pitcher to chill. The can would be half open. Why half open? I don't know to this day.

What I do know is that I love peaches. Anyone who knows me knows how enamored I am with anything that is peach flavored.

"Don't stick your hand in the peach can. Wait until the morning, and we'll have them then." That was her admonition to me every night. The temptation would drive me crazy.

One night, I decided that I would take control. I was so tired of my mother telling me I couldn't have what I desperately wanted. They were just peaches. Good grief! Why did I have to wait till the morning to enjoy them?

In the guise of filling the pitchers, I snuck my chunky finger in the peach can. To my utter disappointment, my finger got stuck and the jagged edge cut my finger. Now blood was oozing into mother's big can of peaches, which she, by the way, thoroughly enjoyed also. I tried my best to get out of the mess I was in by myself, but wisdom eluded me. I had to "fess up" to mother, get her help, and face the discipline for trying to rewrite her rules and get what I wanted.

I think of that incident—so trivial by comparison—when I or other burn survivors I know try to regain control. In our crisis moments, we get so tired of others making decisions for us. Even though they are the professionals, we feel we should have what we want because we want it. The therapist may instruct us to do a series of stretches every day, ten times a day. We say a part of the stretch once a day is enough. It hurts, and I am tired. But when we go back for a checkup, we find that what we did got us in trouble and set us back. Crises come with blinders that impair our better judgment for a space of time. Sometimes it is imperative for others to be in control. It keeps us from harming ourselves.

It's true. We are not always in the right frame of mind to make wise decisions. When I awoke from the coma intubated, the first thing I wanted was the tube to be removed. I think it disturbed me that this large object was lodged in my throat, and I wasn't even asked if I wanted it. If the doctor had asked me if I wanted it removed, I am sure, as stubborn as I am, I would have told him yes—even if he explained I needed it to breathe. My husband tells me that the hospital staff had to tie my hands because I removed it twice while I was in a coma. For my survival's sake, it was good for me not to be in control of that particular decision.

My surgeon was a short, older, easygoing man who happened to be the medical director on the burn unit. His bedside manner was flawless. I liked him instantly. I was told that he was one of the most respected burn surgeons in the nation. I felt God had handpicked this doctor especially for me. He took the time to talk to me about how I was feeling, both body and spirit. His visits weren't rushed.

If I had not known better, I would have thought I was his only patient. I got the sense that he was really listening and that he actually cared. When he had something serious to tell me, he would sit in a chair across from me, cross his leg, rest his chin in his hand, tilt his head slightly, and make direct eye contact.

I remember the day he came to discuss what could be done for my hands. My hands had sustained the most severe injury. The back of my hand and palms had third-degree burns, and I had lost all the skin. My right hand was contorted in an odd "c" shape, and my left hand was mangled and twisted. Most of my fingertips looked like miniature, used charcoal briquettes.

Dr. Parks took both of my hands into his and examined each of them, both back and palm. Then he focused on my right hand.

"Tina," his tone was serious, "it looks like we are going to have to trim your fingers."

I wasn't exactly sure what trimming fingers meant, but I knew it meant I was being scheduled for another surgery.

"Dr. Parks, how many surgeries will I have to have?"

He gave the only honest answer: "I don't know."

By that time, I had already had fifteen surgeries that I could remember. I was so downcast at the news of having another surgery that I never asked him to clarify what trimming my hand meant.

Surgery was performed the next day, and the "trimming" was done. I was wheeled back to my room, groggy as usual.

When Dr. Parks came the next day and unwrapped my hands to take a look at my right hand, I was mortified. My fingers looked like thick, jumbo-sized Vienna sausages. The top section of all four fingers on my right hand had been amputated.

To me, *trimming* was like clipping nails; *amputation* was akin to chopping something off. There was a world of difference between these words. I felt deceived. Amputation was a scary experience; it permanently removed a part f my body.

Dr. Parks explained that the amputation had to be done in order to spare my hand. Again, I was not in control.

A NOTE TO BURN SURVIVORS

The best remedy is to take control of that which you can. Deciphering what you can and cannot change is critical. Any decisions that you can make, make them. The decision can be as small as choosing to sleep on your right side or left. Choice is empowering; it gives you the sense that it is still *your* life.

It is also important that whatever procedures, surgeries, or treatments you are receiving are clear to you. It is imperative to understand what is going on. When you are in the fog about what's happening to you in such a vulnerable stage, the loss of control is amplified. We have heard the old adage that "the only dumb question is the one that is not asked." This is especially true in this complex situation.

Never take for granted a sound mind nor underestimate the power of your will. In particular, never underestimate a will that is coupled with God's will. When my structured world began to break down, my will became the anchor for my survival. Love for my family gave me strength to flow upstream, against the currents of adversity. Paul said in 2 Timothy that "God hath not given us the spirit of fear; but of power, and of love, and a sound mind" (1:7). Fear was shadowing me the whole time as I struggled to gain control of my emotions and faith. By the grace of God, I managed to keep the shadow behind me.

Another tactic I used to steady myself in this not-in-control situation was one that small children use all the time: my imagination. When the situation at hand was heavy and painful to bear, I would lighten my load by planning what I would do when the tide changed. I remember looking at my hands, thinking, *There is no way in the world I will be able to use these again.* But I wanted to. My will was to take care of my family without assistance, and that required the use of my hands. So, I would daydream about the first meal I would cook when I got better, or I would imagine designing the next outfit to sew for my boys.

Cooking Thanksgiving dinner was my first long-term goal. I could smell Butterball turkey with poultry seasoning and sage dressing, mixed greens, buttery corn on the cob, and my secret recipe for mac and cheese. Of course, the meal wouldn't be complete without momma's homemade wheat rolls and cranberry sauce. I was so exhausted from my overactive imagination and the work it would take to make this meal that I decided the kids would do dessert.

As ridiculous as it sounds to be lying on my sickbed mentally cooking a challenging meal, it accomplished two powerful things. First, it stirred up hope. Where there is no hope, there is no effort. Hope ushered in the physical and mental power I needed to climb the difficult terrain I was facing. It had a domino effect. I wanted to cook that meal, so I needed my hands. I needed my hands, so I had to do the therapy. I had to do the therapy, so I had to endure the pain. I had to endure the pain, so I was faithful to take the meds. I had to take the meds, so I was faithful to eat—even when I felt too depressed to do so.

Seven months later, to my family's delight, I cooked that meal. I only had the use of one hand. It was difficult. But it was a sweet victory.

Bless the hand that prepared this food.
–Joseph Page

The second result of this daydream is that it put me back in the driver's seat. My dreams and visions were not controlled by circumstances or conditions. This enabled me to keep a positive attitude more often than not. No matter what was happening around me, I dreamed my dream. Whether or not the grafts took or my blood pressure was low or the splint had to be changed, I could still plan.

Joseph Page delivering Thanksgiving baskets

I made short-term plans and long-term plans. I hated being confined to the bed with the scenery restricted to four white walls, so one of my short-term plans was to be able to sit in a chair. I knew if I could sit in a chair, then I could be wheeled outside my door where I could see activity. I could then make decisions and have interactions based on the activity I saw. In other words, I would have choice and more control of my social interactions.

Before I was able to sit in the chair, my interactions were limited to those who would come and look down at me on my bed. Even though I could request a visitor, the reality was I could not control if he or she would actually show up. Being in the chair outside the room gave me the awesome opportunity to *be* the visitor. Interacting with other patients and their family members provided strength for the journey.

Many aspects of your predicament cannot be changed; we have no choice but to yield to that which is out of our control. No matter how desperately I wanted to go home and teach and take care of my children, I simply could not. I had to acquiesce to the solution I was offered. Two of my sisters in Christ stepped up to the plate to care for my children. Sheila did the everyday motherly duties, and Lori assumed the homeschool schedule. I had to yield and allow them to do what I felt I was called to do.

Yielding can be a rewarding experience and should not be confused with quitting. Yielding affords you time and opportunity to gain strength so that you might take the reins again. Quitting is the abandonment of hope. When you don't hope, you soon don't care. When you don't care, you are treading on dangerous turf. Someone else then becomes the guardian of your circumstances.

It is so important to filter the company you keep during this delicate phase in your life. When you feel out of control, the last thing you need is someone with a negative attitude taking control. I was surrounded by believers who prayed. They were careful to balance a positive attitude with reality. There was no superficial conversation. When the day was sad and depressing, we wept together. When there was good news or a particular triumph, we rejoiced together. They went with the flow. It was a blessing to be surrounded by people who did not force me to have any particular emotion.

Time can be a friend and a bridge to greater control if you allow it. A hospital volunteer visited me on the unit every Saturday. He stood out because, even though he was a stranger, he was faithful to visit every week. He was a tall, older burn survivor who always had a broad smile and cowboy hat in tow. He would ask me how things were going, see if he could assist me with anything, and leave me with the same counsel every time he visited. I can still see Gary leaning against the door frame, holding up his three thick fingers, and saying, "Remember, Justina, you have to do three things: eat, drink, and do what you are told. That's eat, drink, and do what you are told. And don't forget these three words: it takes time." Gary was right on. It does take time to regain control. Time is a friend because time brings change. In time, I wasn't intubated, and I was able to express my desires. In time, I was able to use my hands. In time, I was at home where I wanted to be with my husband and children.

A NOTE TO BURN VICTIMS

Loss of control should not be ignored. It should be acknowledged, addressed, and worked through. Who should acknowledge it? First, you. Pretending won't cut it. Second, others. Reaching out for help is critical. I began to confide in close friends about my fears, anger, and hurt. Therapists and spiritual advisers can help you work through your problems. When the ground is falling from beneath your feet, you need a hand to hang on to. A confidant is priceless during this time.

One day after I was released from the hospital, I was sitting in the living area on my comfortable, green striped couch, watching my friend clean Benjamin's trachea tube. Both of my hands were in splints at that time, and all I could do was watch as she worked.

Benjamin, with his feisty personality, managed to pull out the trachea tube. As Sister Cotton struggled to put it back in, it was evident that he could not breathe. We called 911, and the paramedics were there in record-breaking time.

Benjamin was on his way to the hospital before I could get a grip on what was happening. There I sat, alone, waiting on a ride to the hospital, no longer in control and utterly devastated. I needed help walking and couldn't use my hands. This situation required speed; I was slow and had to be left behind.

Soon Sister Austin arrived to take me to the emergency room and walked in on me sobbing like a baby. She was in shock. She had never seen me cry before.

She even said she didn't know I cried. The tough exterior I displayed and the aura of control I emitted had worked against me.

My child was dying before my very eyes, and she didn't know I cried. What? That was a great "aha" moment for me. It was traumatizing for her to see me out of control.

In the midst of this battle, I chose to trust and lean on the one who is ultimately in control: God. I believed, and still believe, that nothing can happen beyond his knowledge.

Do I feel that he causes every event in our lives? No. We are not robots. We are human beings made in his image who have been given free will and choice. Do I agree with the choices God makes or the things he allows? Most of the time not. But I have learned to yield.

In my yielding, I have discovered he has more wisdom than I do. Life happens to each and every one of us. Life deals us a hand over which we have little control, but how we play that hand is up to us.

Prayer

Heavenly Father, I come to you in the name of Jesus.

I am angry, hurt, fearful, torn, and confused about my situation.

I am not sure if I will make it or if anything will be right ever again.

Nothing is the way I would like it to be.

I feel like you have forsaken me.

My faith is wavering. Lord, I believe, but help my unbelief.

I have lost all control, but I know that you are in control.

I can't do anything for myself, but I know you can do all things.

I wish it didn't have to be this way.

Nevertheless, not my will, but thy will be done.

I want to let patience have her perfect work.

Please show me your purpose in this.

What vision do you have for my life?

I ask that you grant wisdom and strength to my visitors.

If possible, don't let anyone visit my room with discouragement or negativity.

Watch over my husband, children, and family during this crisis.

Help my husband to be strong and to endure the load he has to carry.

Please help me to regain strength physically and spiritually.

I don't want to be a burden.

I know your eye is on the sparrow, and you care for me.

Remember me.

In Jesus' name,

Amen.

Chapter 5

FEAR AND ANXIETY

Life has taken a horrible turn for the worse.

I t has been five days since I have awakened to a living hell. I know that the tank visit will take place sometime this morning. The nurses will load me on the cart and wheel me to the debriding room—the place where hospital staff takes off your burned, dead, and/or infected skin. Basically, they are skinning you alive. They will lower me into the tank, aka, the torture chamber. Their faces will be compassionate. They know this will hurt badly, but they must do what they have to.

After the first few milligrams of morphine are administered, a deceitful peace comes over me, but this feeling quickly dissipates with the first scrub. The soft whimpers of burn patients, anxious about their own tank visits, are heard in the distance. Everyone is dreadfully afraid. My family members and friends are also

33

afraid. They are careful not to say it, and they want to protect me from it, but I see it deep in their eyes. The eye gate gives a premium view into the human soul. I am afraid also—very afraid.

I cannot communicate the depths of my despair and anxiety. I cannot speak nor move. I can only lie there, enveloped in a blanket of dread, tied down by a mass of lines and tubes, wondering, *What type of existence is this? Who can help me? Where is my God?*

My earliest memory of fear is of an incident that occurred when I was three years old. I lived with my great grandmother in Omaha at that time. My great grandmother was fond of antiques. Everything in her house was huge, or at least it seems that way in my memory.

One of her daily tasks was to weed and pick vegetables from her garden on the side of the house. This was a time of sheer delight for me. I hated walking through those weeds and being bitten by those yucky bugs, but a trip to the candy store across the street always followed work in the garden, without fail.

I gladly grabbed my basket, a miniature version of great grandmother's, and happily walked to the field. I was shadowing her as she finished picking the green beans. We were headed to the tomato patch when I first heard it—a hissing, slithery sound. I had no idea what I was hearing. My great grandmother tensed. Her grip on my hand tightened.

"What's wrong?" I asked in a slightly frightened voice.

"Nothing," she said as her eyes searched the perimeter of the garden.

We continued walking, more slowly than before. Out of nowhere, the longest garden snake I had ever seen in my life appeared right in front of us. Even though they are supposedly harmless, it was a monster in my eyes.

We all scattered in different directions: me, great grandma, baskets, vegetables, and even the snake. I don't know who was more afraid, the snake or us. My great grandmother and I eventually found each other in the house.

What I want to point out in relation to the fire was my response to that fear: running. Even at three years old, I knew to run. I didn't know how fast, and I didn't even know where I was going until I got there. I ran until I found a place where I felt safe, a place where the fear and threat were subdued.

I had a similar response when I woke from the coma. I was afraid. I ran, even though my body could not move. Anxiety and anger were making my mind run a marathon. I finally found a resting place in guilt. Not the safest place, but it was my place of choice.

When fear grabs hold of our hearts, most of the time we don't know where we are going or where we should go. We just know that we need to move.

This is what is known as the fight-or-flight response. When we perceive a physical or psychological threat, an automatic reflex, a built-in alarm system, releases electrical impulses and hormones, like adrenaline, that give us extra strength and speed in a threatening situation. This was the response my husband had when he pulled three-quarter-ton air conditioning units from the windows with his bare hands to rescue his family from the flames.

I had never been separated from my children before. We went to parties, sleepovers, and outings together. Even though I knew they were being well taken care of, I still worried. Big worries, small worries, many worries encased me in a web of anxiety. I had proudly taken on the responsibility of motherhood. I gave up my life as I knew it to attend to their needs, both physical and spiritual. When one of my sons hurt his knee, I rubbed it with alcohol and bandaged it. When they were hungry, I prepared the meal. When someone needed to talk, I listened.

Now I could not bandage, prepare, or listen. What was really going on with my children? Will Jonathon be given the responsibilities and challenges he so loved mastering in a day? He doesn't have Amos to look after anymore. Will he be allowed to look after Daniel? Will anyone think to restart Joseph's airplane collection?

Joseph is a thinker. What are his thoughts about us? Joseph doesn't disclose pain easily. Would anyone know when he is hurting?

Is anyone holding Caleb, the most sensitive of the boys? I know he wants his mother. My thoughts went to Daniel, my autistic son. Who knows how to get into his world besides me? Will they watch him closely? He has a tendency to run

Right: Daniel Page enjoys a pet therapy group

Left: Jonathon Page at The Amos House of Faith 2010 Gala

Above: Joseph Page at friend's wedding

Left: Caleb Page working on a new story

off and get into things. He is unable to communicate verbally. Who understands what he wants and what he's feeling the way I do?

Benjamin—I am desperately anxious and fearful to see Benjamin. My emotions about Ben are unstable and divided. The thought of Ben sets off a battle within me. Benjamin is the son who is fettered with me in this excruciating existence. I am elated that he survived and deflated by concern

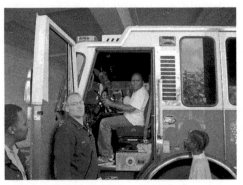

for his quality of life. I have a desire to see him every day, but can't bear the thought of seeing him in pain. He is a constant reminder of what I have and what I have lost. He is a diametrical icon of jubilance and mourning. He is a twin. Ben always followed Amos. Will he follow Amos in death?

The worst type of fear is the prolonged type. This kind of fear fills the space of imminent doom. You fear the unknown, but you know it is going to happen anyway, whatever it is.

In her last years, the family moved my great grandmother from Omaha, Nebraska, to Kansas City, Missouri. I was so attached to her. I had spent the first five years of my life under her care. About five years after the move, she became deathly ill. I was not told that, but I came to my own conclusion after putting two and two together. I was not allowed to go to the hospital.

Every day, I would lie on my grandmother's couch and wait, consumed with fear and waiting for the inevitable. The terror and anxiety stretched over three agonizing weeks. I would take a bath, brush my teeth, get my pillow, and lie down in the same spot. Listening to conversations the adults were having in hopes of overhearing updates, I hoped for the best, feared the worst, and tried to piece together an eight-year-old's image of what was going on. The picture was raggedy.

Finally, the call came that I feared the most. I could tell by the way hands begin to fly to mouths, with just a look. My mother set me up to break the news to me. The words flew out of my mouth before I could rein them in.

"She's dead. She's gone."

"Don't be afraid," my mother said.

As the tears slid down my face, I thought, *I am not afraid anymore.* Fear had held me captive during the wait. What I experienced after the fact was debilitating grief.

That's the sort of fear I was arrested by with Benjamin. I assumed his departure would soon follow Amos's. It was a tormenting existence, especially during the first two weeks after I woke up from the coma. I would actually brace myself for the news every time anyone came to the room. Sitting and waiting and imagining the worst is a horrible pit to fall into.

While visiting me one day, my pastor told me that everything was going to be all right. Those were some of the most comforting words in the world to hear. They were words I desperately needed to hear; they were effective, like a soothing, medicated balm over an irritated sore. He planted a seed of faith that blossomed and chased away my fear of Benjamin's passing.

When I was a teenager, many of my close friends enjoyed going to scary movies and to haunted houses. I thought it was crazy. Why in the world would you go and purposely get the living daylights frightened out of you? It made no sense to me whatsoever. Take me to see a comedy or to watch someone fall in love. Even a mystery that was hard to solve entertained me. But a gruesome experience where you close your eyes every ten seconds, one that left you jumpy and up with nightmares the following week? I just didn't get it.

One time I was with a small group of about eight friends who had decided to go to the movies. When we got to the theater, the movie we planned to see was sold out. With one mind, the group decided to see *Terminator*. Whether it was *Terminator 1* or *2* or *3*, I don't remember. All I know was that I had the choice to sit in the foyer of the cinema and wait or go in with them.

One of the guys persuaded me to go in, even though I tried to explain to him that I wasn't ready for a scary movie. He volunteered to sit by me and sarcastically said he would protect me. I tried to make him understand that this was no joke. I was seriously afraid. He laughed and said he would be glad to hold me.

I looked at him for a heartbeat and then said, "Okay, I warned you."

I've never seen an angrier teenager in my life than he was after the movie. Rightfully so. I had probably burst his left eardrum, considering how loudly I screamed through the whole movie. He had what looked like white claw marks up and down his arm, neck, and the left side of his face. His skin was pierced.

When our group met in the foyer again, they looked at his face and then at me. They were stunned.

All I could do was throw my hands up in surrender, shrug my shoulders, and say, "I told him I wasn't ready."

If only I had experienced as much clarity about how much I could handle with matters concerning Benjamin.

The child life specialist had just left my room. The staff had tried their best to prepare me for my first visit with Ben. They wanted to make sure I was mentally geared up to see him. I already knew I wasn't physically able to hold him, but

I felt as if the opportunity to lay eyes on him would mend forty-two days of painful separation.

The looks on their faces as they left disclosed their doubts about my readiness to see Ben. Nevertheless, my insistence on seeing my son left them little room to do otherwise. They said that they would be returning shortly, pulling Ben in a little red wagon. When I heard the clankety-clank sound of the wagon wheels against the hospital floors, my heart soared. I was finally going to see my baby!

The long, black handle came in view—and I fainted.

When I came to, one thing was painfully clear. I was not ready. When the front of the wagon rounded the corner of my hospital room and I saw the little boy wrapped in gauze and Kerlix bandages on his face and upper extremities, I could not take it.

For the first time, the reality dawned on me that Ben was a patient. He had been burned and burned badly. My son was going through the same pain and suffering that I was. I had been told these things, but reality slammed into me when I saw it. My fear, pain, and anxiety doubled as I realized my child was enduring the same suffering I was going through.

Questions began to plague me: Are they changing Ben's dressings on time? Are they being delicate with him? What if he can't breathe or if he's in pain? How are they managing his pain? How do they know how he feels or what he needs? My anxiety and fear over the whole situation kicked into overdrive. For the next two weeks, I was a serious mess.

I learned a valuable lesson about fear during that time: fear requires faith. It is just faith in reverse. Faith has a positive connotation. We draw from it when we want something improved or something good to happen or when we are looking for the best. Fear is believing the worst and waiting on the manifestation of that.

The common thread in both faith and fear is the unknown. In situations where we don't know the answer, we have an innate prompting to believe something. It took just as much faith to believe that the burn staff on the pediatric unit wasn't equipped to take care of Ben as it did to believe they were.

I've since made it a habit to choose to believe the best in any situation, especially when I don't know what to believe. If it could go one way or the other, why waste energy believing the worst? Ben could make it or not. I eventually got to the point where I saw him living.

Our pastor taught us that our emotions are like children. They should be trained and parented. They should not control us. What a powerful revelation! What an awesome position you are in when you are able to do it. When you are under stressful, painful, and difficult circumstances, your sensitivity is naturally heightened. Emotions can be deep and genuine, yet so fickle.

Someone can make a simple comment, and you can feel encouraged beyond measure. Change one or two words in that comment, and you can feel *discouraged* beyond measure.

A close friend came by to visit one day when an occupational therapist was bending my fingers, an excruciating process. She set the apple juice she had bought for me on my serving table.

"You are really bending those fingers better." Her statement inspired hope. One of my greatest fears was that I would not be able to use my hands again.

A short time later, another friend walked in, set chocolates on the serving table, and leaned close to watch the therapist work. After a few seconds she turned to me.

"You are really bending those fingers better than they said you would." Her words inspired fear. What had the doctors said? Did the doctors say I wouldn't be able to use my hands? Is the pain I'm going through in vain? Are they planning to amputate my hands?

The five little words the second visitor added flipped me from hope to fear. In reality, both friends were trying to communicate the same thing.

A Note to Caregivers

Burn survivors arrive in the burn unit fearful and in agonizing pain. Few things are more intimidating than to be confined to a bed with everyone looking down at you. If there are chairs in the room, sit down. Try to connect emotionally. Take your time, and let the conversation flow naturally. Validate the patient's feelings if he chooses to share them with you. If you are also a burn survivor, make an emotional connection by sharing your experience when he is ready to hear it. Position yourself to offer whatever help he needs.

Fear doesn't always make sense. It is occasionally irrational. Yet even the most irrational fear has a thread of reality in it. And the most rational people have behind-the-scenes fear.

My most piercing, irrational fear during my recovery was fear of divorce. I had not told that to anyone. I did not regard it for a long period of time, but it had a place nonetheless. I had a hidden fear of being left alone. It was irrational because all the signs indicated that my husband loved me unconditionally; he made time to visit me every day.

James's actions and words oozed with love and commitment. I was aware of the depth of his love and faithfulness. So why and what did I fear? I feared the day that he would get tired of the whole situation, the day that enough would be enough, his breaking point. Every human has one. I feared the day would come that he wouldn't want to see or touch one more burn or scar.

I had nothing to offer. I could do nothing for him as a wife. I was needy physically, spiritually, and emotionally. I feared that the load would become too heavy for him. I feared the day that a woman who could help him emotionally or otherwise would catch his eye. He would need an outlet, and an unintended affair would result. I feared my response and the rage that would surely follow.

I had given him the best years of my life—the young, tender, slender days. I feared being abandoned in my older age. Thank God my fear was unfounded. I never told him about my fears, for two simple reasons: the load he was bearing was already heavy, and if I was by chance correct, I did not want to rush the process.

I was freed from this tormenting fear through a decision. I had to trust him and trust God to bear him up. Trusting when you are so vulnerable and are at a disadvantage is no easy task. It is like having your heart wide open and giving the person standing over you a sharp knife along with the power to do what he will. Scary stuff. I didn't have any facts and couldn't prove anything was amiss.

The real power that the fear had over me was the unknown. I reached back and grasped a principle that a friend taught me long ago. When you don't know what to believe, believe the best. I was greatly rewarded for making that decision.

I also had fears that I was embarrassed to talk about. I especially feared nighttime. Nights were horrible for me. My fear and anxiety could be shut out in the bustle of the day. At night, there were fewer distractions. It was a quiet time when dread was amplified, and no one was around to help me fight it. Sometimes I would just cry.

It seemed as though everything fear uttered became law at night. I would sometimes call my husband under the pretense of checking on him and the kids. I wished I had the courage to tell him the truth: I am afraid!

Don't be embarrassed about your fears. Find someone you trust to confide in. Eventually, I gained the courage to confide in an old friend. We were able to battle my fear at night together, and that connection provided a sweet relief.

Fear makes me remember being frightened, scared, and in the dark.
At the end, I want to be saved. No more nightmares.
—**Patrick Edwards Jr.**, 11, After Burns Club member and burn survivor

Anxiety opposes healing. You have to tackle anxiety head on in order for healing to progress faster. I was so anxious about my kids. I was used to being in control; not knowing what was going on was driving me crazy.

My good friend Sheila took over the care of my children. We had met in college, and both of our families had moved to Houston and joined the same church. I trusted her implicitly. She was a woman known for her love for people, especially children. She was familiar with my standards and routines and did her best to do what I would do.

Out of all the many wonderful things she did for me, the most important was when she began to give routine reports on what was going on with my children. It eased my anxiety dramatically. Wherever your anxiety lies, combat it with education. Become as informed as you can; anxiety ferments in the unknown.

Anxiety is counterproductive. You never get the solutions or results you need with it. It has an accomplice; anxiety's twin brother is worry. They look alike but serve two distinct purposes. Anxiety is triggered by the feeling of uneasiness over a real or imagined situation. Anxiety takes a great deal of creativity on the anxious person's part.

Worry, on the other hand, has a basis it's built on. The basis may be solid or not. Worry does tend to follow anxiety. I was anxious about Ben, extremely anxious. I was uneasy about how he was really doing. My imagination did not help. I took the things that I was experiencing and magnified them ten times worse. I was worried about the other boys. The basis was simple. I was their primary caregiver. No one else had ever had ever taken care of them before.

My greatest weapon against fear was faith. When fear would carry me to the end of my rope, I would remember who I was and who I believed in. Faith gave me a platform to stand on when the ground beneath me had given away. I believed God would never leave me. I had to trust him. Fear moves you to ally yourself with something; God was the best choice for me.

Prayer

Heavenly Father, I come to you in the name of Jesus.
Please help me. I am so afraid, especially now at nighttime.
I don't think I am going to make it. I don't know what to believe.
What about my children, Lord?
Are they really okay?
Please watch over and protect them.
I am so anxious about them. I am sure they are afraid too.
Comfort them for me.
Will my husband be able to endure this storm?
Give him strength and wisdom. I love him.
I know that you told us to be anxious about nothing, but by prayer and
supplication to make our request known unto you.
You also said that you have not given us a spirit of fear,
but of power and of love and a sound mind.
I want to stand on your promises.
I will believe you and not fear.
Thank you for your promises and your peace.
In Jesus' name,
Amen.

Chapter 6

REALIZATION OF LOSS

Wait! I remember something—someone didn't
make it! Lord, no! I've lost a child!

emories are assaulting me in my sleep, taunting me, mocking
me: picnics, birthday parties, school, antique furniture, children
laughing, children screaming, sirens, and darkness. Wait! I
remember something—someone didn't make it! Lord, no! I've lost a child!

The loss is so huge and devastating that it overshadows all other losses. I can
no longer remember losing all the furniture, clothes, or any material possession.
My losses are real and not just a figment of my imagination.

Coming to terms with loss is painful because it ushers in an unwanted
distress called grief. You cannot realize loss without feeling pain. I couldn't think
of Amos without feeling as if a grenade was being set off within me. It hurt, and
it hurt badly.

Amos Beniah Page

Today, Benjamin is a constant reminder of that loss. When I look at Ben, I can't help but wonder if Amos would be so tall. Would Amos like soccer and playing on the computer? Would Amos be crazy about apples and grapes like Ben?

Every morning, I am forced to realize that same loss over and over again. But as I heal and allow time to exchange sorrow for purpose, the continued realization of the loss has a less sorrowful effect.

I was a scholar athlete and a well-rounded student—an ultimate overachiever. In high school, I played basketball and volleyball, ran track, and played in the band. I was also head cheerleader for four years, in the honor society, math club, and on the dissection team. My outside activities included the tumbling team, tap, jazz, ballet, baton, and leading the drill team. I enjoyed being involved.

When I went to college, I cut back on my activities but still continued with basketball and joined the gospel choir. I had a slew of memory books, medals, trophies, and pictures that I wanted to share with my children when they got into their teenage years. I am sentimental and had kept letters from friends, notes, and all sorts of memories. The fire destroyed them all. It was a devastating blow.

I wanted to give my children a peephole into my teenage years as they were experiencing theirs. Some things that are lost cannot be recovered. Now, all I could do was try to transfer verbally a few glimpses into my childhood.

We took our first family vacation after the fire in December of 2000. I wanted to make it extra-special in light of all the things the kids had been through. I ordered twenty VHS tapes and fifteen games that they had never seen before. I bought each child his own separate luggage set, toiletries, and brush. I scored major brownie points for that one. I packed every ball, toy, and book we could find, and then we hit the road.

We stopped at the outlet mall in San Marcus along the way. The boys got their treat, Nikes, and I got mine—purple everything. We had a timeshare in the

San Antonio hill country that we refused to let go to waste. It was a two-story, three-bedroom condo tucked in a mountain side with a view toward the lake.

I was able to cook when I wanted to, and we ate out when I didn't. It was a wonderfully convenient space for a family of eight on vacation. It provided us enough space to do family activities as well as enough seclusion for my husband and me to have private times together. We went on to San Antonio and stayed at a hotel. We had no choice but to make sure that Joseph got his chance to experience the Aviation Museum. We went on to the River Walk, the Alamo, and several other tourist attractions.

We were on our way to the IMAX theatre in the River Walk Mall when I got sidetracked. There before me stood the most beautiful sight in the world: The Purple Store. I had never heard of such a place. The boys let out an audible gasp. "Oh, no," they groaned in unison as they covered their faces and shook their heads. I shrieked with delight.

My husband took the boys on a short excursion while I lived my dream. We took an assortment of pictures and recorded every detail of the trip. The boys sang all the way home.

A week later, I took the opportunity to reminisce about the trip. My husband was at work, and all the boys were at school except Benjamin. He was distracted by the toy he was playing with. I took the tape that was labeled part one of four, San Antonio trip, and slipped it in the VHS player. The trip came to life instantly.

It was strange; I didn't feel the excitement I remembered. In fact, a great sorrow enveloped me. The more I watched, the more sorrowful I felt. Then it dawned on me. Subconsciously, I was looking for and grieving for Amos. I wanted him to be there. It was our first family trip that he was not a part of. I ran to the den and got the pictures of the trip. As I flipped through them, I wept like a baby.

My mind was playing tricks on me. It was as if we forgot to take Amos with us. I wanted to go back and do it all over again, to make sure Amos was in the car. As the realization of the loss surfaced, I became sick to my stomach. Amos would never take another family trip with us. His last family trip was in 1998 when we went to Washington, DC.

A friend in Kansas City bought my firstborn the most adorable dinosaur outfit I had ever seen. It was black and white, checkered on the left side and on both arms. On the right side was an oversized red dinosaur with a glass eye. The matching hat had red, triangular pieces on the top.

At three months, each child was photographed in that outfit. We would do our standard family portraits every year at JCPenney or Olan Mills. The set had to include a picture of all the boys alone, a picture of Mom and her boys, a picture of Dad and his sons, and finally the couple that had produced this flock.

I especially liked taking photos of real-life moments. At home I would shoot priceless snapshots of Jonathon feeding Caleb, Joseph concentrating on his model airplane, Daniel sneaking cookies, or Amos and Benjamin playing church. I had more photo albums than I had places to keep them. When you can't recall certain events, pictures fill in the gap to remind you. So many memories were lost in that fire.

The boys have a few pictures that capture their adolescent years. Family members and friends were compassionate and gave us their photos of our family so we could have a few earlier memories. When your attempt to preserve your children's memories is thwarted, it can be heartbreaking.

All but one of the photo albums was destroyed in the fire. In the midst of the charred debris, our wedding album was recovered. The lavender satin on the outside cover was burned and water-stained beyond recognition. The pretty plum bow was missing, but the pictures inside that captured some of the happiest memories in our lives remained untouched. The smell of smoke was potent, but the pictures weren't even water damaged.

It was apparent by looking at the outer cover that it had been through a fire. But pulled out of the album, the pictures appeared to be unscathed. To me, the pictures symbolized our ability to stay intact.

In the end, God had allowed us to go through the fire with only the visible burns and scars to testify of our journey. The inner person had returned to the faith and strength that it was so comfortable with.

Most people remember where they were on September 11, 2001, the day Al-Qaeda terrorists carried out suicide attacks on US soil, changing forever the way Americans look at security. Talk about a national feeling of loss of control.

When it happened, I had been at my son's middle school for no more than ten minutes. It was a field trip day. I was one of the brave parents that signed up to chaperone a group of unruly middle schoolers. They are called VIPs—volunteers in public schools. I was signing in at the VIP kiosk when I looked up and saw the school TV monitor. A plane had crashed into a tall building.

I'm pretty opinionated, so I had to ask what was going on. In an irritated voice, I asked the registrar at the desk, "Excuse me. What type of violence are we feeding the kids around here?"

It took her a few minutes to realize I was talking to her.

"Can you believe this?" She was obviously perplexed about something. "Someone just flew a plane straight through the North Tower of the World Trade Center."

What? That was *real?* I was temporarily stunned. I did an about face and went to the attendance office to withdraw my son from the school. If people were flying planes into buildings, I wanted all my children with me. I needed to be in control.

As I went from school to school to gather everyone up, I felt the folly of having five kids in five different schools. Taking my children out of school was an attempt to bring something under control. I had temporarily lost trust in government protection. I didn't know what was going to happen next. When it did, I wanted my kids to be under my wings.

Trauma can have a similar effect. You need to grab on to something. Your sense of security has been compromised. You don't know what is going to happen next.

When I did finally make it home, my husband was there also. He was scheduled to go to Florida the next day to look at a project. One striking detail dawned on us at the same time: the last-minute trip to Florida had forced him to cancel his flight to New York the previous evening.

My husband and his co-worker had been scheduled to have a nine o'clock meeting in the same tower that had just been obliterated.

All I could do was thank God for his mercy and pray for his co-workers and the many others that were affected by the tragedy.

I instinctively prioritized the multiple losses in my life. It was not until I came to terms with the first major loss that I could even recognize and deal with the next one in line.

The fear of Benjamin and me losing our lives was number one.

When I awoke from the coma on a ventilator and found out Benjamin was in the same shape, I had one thing on my mind: Lord, let us live. After I was past the terror of dying, I was able to focus more fully on losing my son.

Grief is an intuitive response to loss. The grieving time varies with the type of loss and the potential for recovery. Some losses cannot be regained. I had lost health and strength, but now I am healthy and no longer grieve for life. I had lost a home, a car, and many possessions. I no longer grieve over them because they have been replaced.

But the loss of Amos is a completely different story. I will likely go to my grave grieving for my son.

We lost a lot of things in that fire.
—Caleb Page

Caleb hit the nail on the head when he expressed his sense of loss. It has been years now, and I still occasionally recall something else that we lost in the fire. Of course, Caleb was thinking of his toys, books, videos, and clothing. We each had our separate list of things we lost that affected us the most. I would always tell Caleb and the other boys the same thing over and over again: Don't focus on the loss. Acknowledge it, cry about it, but don't let it carry you to a bad place.

It is amazing how simple an instruction seems when you are giving it. But when you turn around and have to act on the words you are dispersing, it can be bitter. I loved stuffed animals—all sizes, shapes, and kinds. By the time I got to college, my collection was quite impressive. I had a special group of stuffed toys within my collection: Smurfs. I loved those little blue elves. I even unashamedly went to college with my twin-sized Smurf comforter set. I had everybody: Smurfette, Clumsy, Dreamy, Brainy, Hefty, Grouchy, the whole gang.

One day I noticed that Smurfette was MIA. She was not in her place in the group. Smurfette happened to be my favorite Smurf. It was the only one that had been given to me as a gift; it came from a persistent suitor. I had a tendency to rearrange my animals every two weeks. I got bored with the same routine. Monotony drives me up the wall. James always told me that he was afraid to buy a house for fear that I would have him remodeling annually. I kept my cool as I searched my small dormitory room. There weren't many places Smurfette could be.

Before I knew it, I was having an all-out panic attack. The loss was devastating. Sure, it was just a stuffed toy and a replaceable one at that. But it wasn't losing the blue fur and golden locks that made me sick. It was the emotional value I placed on the object; what it meant to me emotionally is what hurt the most.

I had similar feelings about the things I lost in the fire. I am not a materialistic person, but everything I had, from the French provincial couch in the front room to the picture my husband drew for me during our engagement, had a priceless value, an emotional attachment.

I wasn't bothered by losing the couch because of the expense and rarity; it was a piece of furniture that reminded me of my great grandmother. If he so desired, my husband could stop and draw me another picture. The first one showed his hand giving me a single red rose. If he wanted to now, he could draw a picture of him showering me with a dozen roses. But the original was the first drawing he ever did for me. Now I had to remember my own words: don't focus on the loss.

I could acknowledge every painful memory associated with losing everything. I could even mourn the loss, but as I told the kids, I had to move on. I could not let the loss take me to a bad place, a place of bitterness and defeat.

So what did I do? I did what comes naturally for me. I started over again and created a whole new set of memories with just as much emotional value and sentiment as the things I had before.

I was in my bedroom, sitting on the oversized wicker chair with my favorite purple, floral-print cushion. I was looking out the glass patio doors, praying about my children's future. A loud thump sounded at the front of the house. It was followed by a group of high-strung little fellows racing to get the mail. Screams of "I got it!" seemed to be coming from every part of the house.

Everything is a competition to my boys. Joseph won, as usual. He was always a bit faster and wittier than the other boys. Joseph entered my room, smiling. "Here's the mail, Mother." Then he raced off to continue his game.

I flipped through the mail absentmindedly until I ran across the letter I was looking for, one from Cigna insurance company. A huge smile filled my face. My husband had just transferred to a new company, and I was anxious for the new insurance cards to arrive so I could find a pediatrician and dentist for the kids.

I opened the letter, pulled out the two plastic cards, set one aside, and examined the other closely. James R. Page Jr. 0091530, Justina R. Page 0091531, Jonathon J. Page 0091532, Joseph J. Page 0091533, Caleb J. Page 0091534, Daniel J. Page 0091535, Benjamin J. Page 0091537. Wait. Why would they go from 35 to 37? Oh, no—36 was Amos! I went totally numb.

Would the loss of Amos manifest itself so blatantly in every aspect of my life? I never said a word to anyone about my reaction to the missing name and number. Perhaps I should have, but I figured that no one else could relate to this the way I did. Everyone knew Amos was gone. Why should I fall into shock because his name was not on the insurance card?

Why it affected me that way is irrelevant. The reality is that it did. What affects you is what affects you. We shouldn't deny it or hide it. The healing begins when we admit it. Admitting it also puts you within arm's reach of help. You would be surprised at the number of people who may be touched by your struggles. They also have a wealth of wisdom and experience to help you along.

The experience with the insurance card struck a chord in my heart. The card seemed to shout, "He is gone! Move on!" My tenacity said, *He will never die in my heart.* From that moment on, I began to jot down memories of him. His journey on earth was brief—only twenty-two months. But he had lived out a full life and developed a distinct personality in those few days. Recalling those memories was soothing and a way to keep him close.

I set aside a Queen Anne curio cabinet to store memories of him. Inside, I have poems that were written about him, pictures, a little boy angel that a child gave me while I was in the hospital, and the program from the funeral. On top, I have a large, framed picture of him with his name and "Rest in Peace" on it. Beside the picture, I like to keep a fresh bouquet of flowers that signifies the continuation of his life with God. At night, I turn on the curio light and sit there and just remember him. I never let him die in my heart.

What constitutes a loss for you may not necessarily be a relevant loss for others—not even to those closest to you. I lost the first joint of my four fingers on my right hand. Do the boys miss the first joint on my four fingers on my right hand? I think not. They still get their dinner prepared and their laundry done on a regular basis. Does my husband miss them? Not likely. The house gets clean and is managed just the same. But I really miss them. Why, you might wonder, especially if I can still do almost everything I did before? I miss them because they were mine.

What am I getting at? The key is I can do almost everything I did before. There are some things I can't do, no matter how simple they seem to be. I can no longer latch a necklace by myself. I need help cutting my meat, at restaurants and at home. Am I bowing and weeping over it? No. But it still doesn't diminish the fact that it is a loss.

The mere fact that I don't look the same as I did before the fire is another example of loss. I am now scarred and amputated. It doesn't matter how people compliment you on how much better the scar looks or how well the burns healed. The image I was accustomed to has been altered. It is a loss worthy of recognition and mourning.

It is natural and healthy for us to mourn for our losses. Mourning is a sign that you have accepted the new reality in which you are living. David elegantly expressed this in the book of Psalms: "Weeping may endure for a night but joy cometh in the morning" (30:5) In other words, mourning has a predetermined existence to live out its days in any situation.

Despite the magnitude of loss I suffered, I am mindful to be grateful for what was left. I have my life and health and strength. I have my husband and five other sons. Many of the material possessions I lost have been replaced. Most precious to me is the reestablishment of my joy, love, peace, and faith in Christ.

I have managed not to let the losses drown out the good memories, especially the times when Amos was with us. I treasure the trips we took to see family in Kansas City and St. Louis, the vacations we took to Washington, DC, and Palestine, Texas. I have even taken it a step further. Now I am determined to create new memories. If you think about it, to experience a loss is a testament to "having had." It is truly amazing how we take for granted what we have. It is like the old adage: you don't miss your water till your well runs dry. In my case the well practically disappeared. Hindsight allows me to see clearly how the life I had prior to the fire was a vessel overflowing with joy, peace, and contentment.

Of course, while I was in the moment, it didn't appear to be so. The temporary loss of the use of my hands was an ideal example of this quandary. My hands were at the beckoning service of six deserving princes and one honorary king. From the moment my eyes were roused open by the rising sun, till the moment I would lie down from an exhausting day, my hands were engaged in activity. I was blinded by the daily tasks of changing diapers, cooking, teaching, and making play dates.

I used to joke about what a blessing it would be not to have hands, foolishly implying that the responsibility on me would be redirected. But when that idea became a reality, I was stumped. It takes a wise person to discern the true meaning of the outburst that is made in times of distress. What I really wanted was the help of those around me. I learned that in a stressful moment, you don't mean half of what you say.

Not all loses are detrimental. Some losses are actually good. With every loss, there is an opportunity to gain. Losing makes gaining all the more precious. You don't always gain what you lost, but gain is gain and will benefit you if you acknowledge it and use it appropriately. I lost a home, a child, and precious mementos, none of which can be recovered. But I gained greater faith, increased wisdom, deeper compassion, lasting friends, and contentment—all of which brings great fulfillment.

Prayer

Heavenly Father, I come to you in the name of Jesus.

The loss seems unbearable. Help me to deal with my loss.

People really don't understand. I don't have anything.

My kids will never see my senior book or view my old basketball tapes.

I wish I had shown it all to them before this.

I want to do like Paul and forget those things that are

behind and press forward to the things that are ahead.

I know that the things I had were given to me by you.

You are a God of increase.

I also know that you can replace many of the things that we have lost.

You are a God of restoration.

I am asking you to grant me the things I especially need:

love, faith, peace, and contentment.

Chapter 7

ANGER

I am furious, and I want answers. Why me?

What did I do to deserve this? Why must I hurt from sun up to sun down? Why do the nurses scrub so hard every morning? Why is everyone pretending everything is going to be okay when we all know I am going to die? I know my husband is faithful and visits every day, but why can't he stay here with me through the night when I am most afraid? Where is Benjamin, and why can't I see him? Will Benjamin die also? Why have I lost any semblance of independence? Why have I lost every earthly possession? Why did I lose my precious son? God? God? You could have stopped this, yet you allowed it! I am furious, and I want answers. Why me?

When I was a sophomore electrical engineering student, James was a junior. I had come to respect him for so many reasons. He was intelligent and a meticulous tutor. When you really wanted to understand the material, you went to him. If you just wanted the answers to the problem, you stayed away.

One time, he called to tell me I had left my Calculus 3 book at his house. I said I would quickly pick it up before he had to leave for class. As he handed me the book, I saw an unusual sparkle in his eyes. I thanked him for the book and turned to leave. He asked if I had time for a quick question.

I turned around, curious about what was going on with him. He dropped to one knee and asked me if I would be the mother of his children. It was the most romantic thing I had ever experienced. I was clearly stunned, and he couldn't interpret my blank stare and hesitation to speak.

He began to assure me that I had plenty of time to answer him, but saying yes was a no-brainer. I felt as if I would burst with joy. I started trying to figure out when and how I was going to let him know I accept. My plan began to take shape while he was still kneeling.

It was the day before his birthday. I hugged him and told him we would talk later. Of course, I skipped class that day to make calls to my besties, to tell them about my proposal. I also began to prepare the extravagant yes I planned to give him on his birthday.

With the help of his roommate, I hid in his room while he was at class the next day. He walked into his house to see twenty-one dove balloons that each said yes and a big birthday cake. The look on his face was endearing. It was settled. I would become Mrs. James Page Jr.

The wording of his proposal revealed his anticipation for fatherhood. Children were our dream and what our lives would revolve around. He was present for every birth and caught every son in his own hands. He was not the least bit concerned about the goopy umbilical fluid. He would bless the child and hand him to me. With each safe birth, our hearts would swell with thanksgiving and love.

Then one day, God took one. Why would God do that? A baby. One of our twins.

God is not fair.
—**Jonathon Page**

Mr. & Mrs. Page Jr. Taking Vow

One angry thought fed into another one: *My son is gone. My son is hurt. My children are traumatized. I can't breathe. I can't walk. I can't use my hands. I'm angry at God. I'm angry at the landlord. I'm angry at the nurse. I'm angry at the therapist. I'm angry at me. I'm angry at the world for going on and not stopping to acknowledge my loss and grieve with me.* The list was growing longer and longer and longer and longer.

But I was a Christian, a woman of faith who had submitted to God's will. I felt I had to deny this forbidden feeling that was gnawing at my heart. But the more I attempted to deny it, the stronger it grew, until eventually it spread. For a brief period of time, I was angry at just about everyone, seemingly about everything and anything.

Anger is the most self-destructive emotion I know. It is a sprinter that causes you to make swift, foolish, harmful moves. For me personally, it is the hardest emotion to manage. I try my best to take every precaution to avoid it. When it comes alive in me, I must deal with it in a hurry. Otherwise, something or someone, me included, will be hurt.

The first day my kids went to public school, after years of being homeschooled, was stressful for me. The school year was 2000-2001. Jonathon was in seventh grade; Joseph was in fifth; Caleb second; and Daniel kindergarten. Just the night before, I was bragging about how nice it would be to get a break, get some rest, and do something for myself. In reality, however, I was on pins and needles that first day, praying and watching the clock. Benjamin was my human security blanket, but even he got tired of my cuddling him and escaped to his room to play.

I remember standing on the porch, looking down the street for the buses. When Jonathon came in, I barely heard his greeting. I was distracted by the long, red scratch that went from the right side of his neck to the center of the back of his neck. Anger gripped me, and I scrambled for control.

"Jonathon," I said in the most controlled voice I could muster, "what happened to your neck?" I knew, of course; I just wanted to get a verbal confirmation so anger could have the right to do what it thought was best.

Jonathon reached across his face and touched the scar with his left hand.

"A boy at school scratched me." His voice was slightly sad.

I could feel the hairs on my neck raise up. I didn't ask for God's help or take a slow, deep breath. Oh, how I wish I had done that now. Anger was in the driver's seat and rage in the passenger seat, buckling themselves in.

"What did you do?" My voice was barely audible.

"Nothing. I turned the other cheek." He was proud of himself.

I was furious. I made a quick eye scan of the house, making sure my husband was not in close proximity. Then I got on one knee, making sure I was at eye level with him, and said the most damaging, irrational thing you could ever tell a child in that situation: "If someone ever touches you again, beat him down to the ground." For that second, I meant exactly what I said.

Anger is demanding, bullish in its execution. Anger commands respect it doesn't deserve. The words spewed out of my mouth, full of the anger and rage that had possessed me.

I got a call from the middle school the next day because Jonathon had broken a student's nose. Now, I'm afraid—not for Jonathon or the injured boy, but for me. I knew that Jonathon's predicament was the result of my hastily given advice to beat people down to the ground. I also knew that my husband would eventually find out what I said. His lovely Christian wife and homemaker—turned boxing instructor—had given ridiculous advice to her son and now two children were in a bad way.

It is the nature of anger to make you step out of character. It coerces you to do embarrassing things that you eventually come to regret. Boy, did I regret that one. Of course, I went to the school to smooth this mess over. I was back-pedaling now. They were compassionate with Jonathon in light of the recent tragedy and present circumstances.

I was waiting for Jonathon to get home so I could exchange the advice I gave him yesterday for something more sensible. I had cooled off and could speak with reason. My husband pulled up right when the bus dropped him off at the corner. Goodness. Now we both were waiting for him. When he walked in the door, his father immediately took him to our bedroom to see why he had broken someone's nose. I purposely stayed in the front room, trying to fathom how I would explain myself. I overheard Jonathon's response: "Mother said if someone hits me, I should beat him down to the ground."

I'm sure my husband was in shock. I was grabbing my keys and purse to make an escape when I heard my husband call for me. He asked the question I knew was surely coming: "Did you tell our son to beat someone down to the ground?" He sounded incredulous.

I was tempted to lie. But instead, I simply said yes.

My husband arched his left eyebrow and gave me an "are you crazy?" stare, then said, "I will talk with you later."

James turned toward Jonathon and began to explain the difference between defending yourself and beating people down to the ground. I was dismissed, head hanging down and covered with shame. This is the posture in which anger generally leaves you when it has had its way.

When you are angry, you can be irrational. The first ICU nurse who tended to me when I came out of the coma was a short, stout man with an easy going manner about him. He walked in my room and began fiddling with the IV pumps and knobs. I was instantly angry with him. He didn't even speak. That was silly of me. I had been in a coma and unable to talk for six weeks.

When he did look at me, he said the dumbest thing ever. "You're awake! How are you feeling?"

Not only is he rude, but he is insensitive too, I thought. I wanted to pull that tube out of my throat and yell, "How in the world do you think I am feeling? Do you think I can really answer you?" My silent outrage was interrupted by his monotone voice.

"Blink your eyes if you can hear me."

I blinked back the tears coming to the forefront. Good. Now what? I don't like him. I want another nurse, but I can't speak, move, or use my hands. I can only respond to his barrage of questions by blinking. No one was asking the questions I wanted answered. Communication was a one way street.

> *It took a long time for me to understand that anger would*
> *get me nothing. It could not save me, protect me, or defend*
> *me. It would never make me happy, strong, or content.*
> —**Cynthia Ash**, Amos House of Faith volunteer and burn survivor

I was finally able to sit up with several pillows propped behind me. My back was killing me, but to be able to look down on something rather than being looked down on gave me a sense of command. My pastor's wife and another sister from my church were in the room, visiting with me. I was really enjoying their company. We were immersed in memories and laughter.

"Can I share something with you that I know?" Sister Jones asked out of the blue.

"Sure." I had a feeling the tone of the visit was being redirected.

She gave me a sympathetic smile and said, "You are very angry. Ask God to help you deal with that."

It was the truth—an inconvenient truth, but the truth all the same. I felt as if the cover had been pulled off and a sacred secret had been exposed. I had to deal with my anger.

My first experience with a destructive storm was with Hurricane Ike in 2008. Even though it was only a category three storm, once it hit land, it was devastating. It came in the middle of the night. In a moment, the weather was transformed from a peaceful calm to a chaotic fury. I had never heard winds so sinister in my life. You could hear the tree limbs breaking.

Benjamin was so frightened that he burst through the bathroom door that joined our rooms and leaped in the bed between my husband and me. A category three storm has sustained winds at more than 110 miles per hour, accompanied by torrential rain. It hit the Houston and Galveston areas with a frightening ferocity.

Ike was angry. Ike shut down 75 percent of the power in the greater Houston metropolitan area in its aftermath. Reinforcements had to be called in from all over the country to help rebuild the power lines; more than two million people were left without electrical power, which was not restored to some areas for more than six weeks.

Hurricanes form in the warm, moist waters of the Atlantic and Pacific oceans near the equator, and the momentum and strength is increased when as the storm continues to travel over warm water. What breaks the intensity and power of the hurricane is cool water and land.

What a perfect analogy for the anger I experienced after the fire. The destructive winds remind me of the uncontrollable thoughts that fueled my fury. The warm, moist waters were the depths of pain that resulted from the devastation that was experienced. The hurricane that results is the damaging acts that are a result of the anger itself. The eye of the hurricane is the subdued reality that there is nothing you can do about your situation. The cool waters are the words of encouragement from others, the compassion and understanding of your supporters.

When we are angry, we have to calm the winds. Our thoughts are a force to be reckoned with. That's why Paul instructed us in the book of Philippians to think about things that are pure, just, lovely, and true (4:8). I've laid in my bed on the burn unit as mad as all get-out about my present situation. And boy, can I get angry and hold it. Most passionate people are like that.

All of that wasted energy was not powerful enough to change one thing about my predicament. What had happened had happened. That part was over. I needed to focus on the next moment. Anger could not assist me with that at all. I had to find my way to the center of my anger, the eye of the storm, the painful place of acceptance.

The top item on anger's agenda is to vindicate itself, to strike back at whatever it feels has stricken at it. It tells us to take vengeance. Even if we succeed to our own satisfaction, it is a futile effort. The effort is fruitless because the core of our inner desire is not fulfilled.

As illogical as it is, admitting your anger can be difficult when you are going through a traumatic situation. After all, it seems you have every reason to be angry. My anger was, however, like a hidden cancer eating away on the inside. I was ashamed of my anger and tried my best to conceal it when people were around. But when I was alone, I nursed my anger and helped it grow. The praises of loved ones and friends concerning my supposedly tenacious faith and strength kept me beaming on the outside, but all the while, I was decaying on the inside.

As long as I hid my feelings and denied my anger, I could not get the help I needed. Admitting my struggles meant that I was not the invincible Christian that I—and everyone else— thought I was. So what? God himself gets angry, right?

My pastor taught us that it is not our actions but our reactions that unveil who we really are. Actions can be thought out and scripted, but reactions are a heart response. Unresolved anger contaminates the heart and taints our responses.

A NOTE TO BURN SURVIVORS

Make sure you express your anger. Address the situation—not in a combative way, but by respectfully sharing how you feel. It is also good to redirect your anger. This can be done by not concentrating on the source of your anger but instead turning to something more constructive. And simply try to calm down. It will reduce the stress, clear your mind, and put you in a frame of mind where you can make wise decisions.

I knew I had to focus on something constructive. I was angry that the fire had mangled my hands and caused me to have a partial amputation, leaving me with no use of my hands. But instead of dwelling on the fire, which I could not change anyway, I began to focus on what it would take to use my hands again.

Although light from the sun appears white, it actually contains a range of colors similar to the rainbow. You can see these colors using a prism to separate them out. Our expectations are like the light from the sun; they seem reasonable, easy to perform, and right. Anger is birthed when our expectations are violated.

The tragedies that befall us are like the prism. When our expectations hit that prism, the flaws in our expectations are manifested in a variety of colors.

I expected every one of my children to grow up and not deal with any trauma whatsoever. I made room for a broken bone or scratched knee, but never death, sickness, and the depth of loss they actually experienced. I did not expect my son to die. I became angry. With whom? First, God. I held him accountable for Amos's death—just as if he came down from heaven in the form of fire and ignited the house. Then I saw that was a foolish judgment, but I was still angry at God for not saving Amos. He could have; I know that.

But God was the one I depended on to carry me through the crisis. It is hard to communicate with and lean on someone with whom you are angry, so I let that go. However, my anger was not assuaged. My anger needed a victim to keep the inferno burning. When we can't strike at God, we go for the next best thing: people we can see and touch. I like the proverb King Solomon wrote, "Where no wood is, there the fire goeth out" (Prov. 26:20). Watch the wood and the wood deliveries when you are in a traumatic situation.

When you are on the burn unit and bedridden, you have a lot of time to think. Sometimes that's a good thing and sometimes not. Have you ever been just about to let go of a negative situation when a visitor came in and brought it up again? After he leaves, your thoughts have changed, and you are back to being angry about that situation all over again. Words spoken by visitors can leave you angrier than you were before they came. A word is a powerful thing for a visitor to bring to your bedside. Practice listening to everything and hearing only the constructive things.

We are instructed in Ephesians 4:26 to be angry yet sin not. Anger doesn't give us the right to hurt others. We must get to the root of our anger so that it will not grow and sprout up into bitterness. We should also avoid conversations that flare our anger. Just as charcoal briquettes can be stirred up to ignite again, anger can be instigated and resurface.

I tried to be upset with a lot of different people, but my real beef was with God. I did not understand why he allowed me to go through such a horrific tragedy. It wasn't long before I began to understand that God does not start fires; he helps you through them. Yet the remarks of others drew me back to that same place of anger: "I don't know why God did this to your beautiful family." "You never know what's going to happen." "How can you keep your faith?"

I was bedridden, so I had no choice but to hear what was said in my room. I tried to filter the conversation swirling around me. I clung to that which was useful and flushed the rest.

When I was first released from the hospital, I still needed assistance with everything—walking, sitting, eating, and going to the bathroom. My husband was at work and the women at my church were taking care of us. The kids were with a special friend from college named Lori who had taken on the responsibility of homeschooling my children. Another friend of mine, Demetria, was taking care of various tasks in the home. I had been helped to the commode and was sitting there, furious. I couldn't get up or even clean myself. It hurt my pride to have to call someone to help me up and clean me. But I had no choice.

I called for Demetria. She came and extended her hand over the wooden "stall" door to hand me a roll of toilet paper to clean myself. She had assumed there were no rolls in there. I remember looking at her hand and the roll thinking, *This is really awkward.*

Then I told her, "That is your job." We must have laughed all day long. The laughter made the situation less awkward, and I felt so much better. Humor became another weapon in my arsenal. It was my weapon of choice to combat anger.

Prayer

Heavenly Father, I come to you in the name of Jesus.

I am so angry with my landlord, the doctors . . . I'm angry with you.

Why did you let this happen? It hurts.

You are God. I can't be angry with you. Please help.

I don't want to make you angry. What did I do?

Help me with my anger.

I don't want to lash out at those who are trying to help me.

I don't want to hurt anyone.

You have allowed us to be angry,

but you don't want us to sin.

I know that grievous words stir up anger.

Please help me to filter the conversation around me.

Send peaceful visitors my way.

Thank you for understanding. I want to do better.

In Jesus' name,

Amen.

Chapter 8

THE PROBLEM OF PAIN

It hurts—body, mind, spirit, and soul.
The pain is strangling me.

I hate the sight of the occupational therapist and the physical therapist. Not so much the individual, but what they represent. I see them as walking, talking torture instruments in the form of human beings, complete with arms and legs. As they approach the room, I try my best to concoct an excuse to get out of the therapy. They are wiser and more experienced than most of us patients. They've heard our schemes a million times over. They afflict pain graciously, often with a smile. To the inexperienced onlooker, it seems to be just a slight bend or touch, no big deal. Onlookers, however, cannot relate to the super sensitivity of exposed, raw nerves or the torture of moving muscles that have not been used for months. What do onlookers know of pain that grips your whole body and refuses to let go?

The session is exhausting. Pain is an intriguing dilemma. Its tentacles intertwine themselves intricately throughout the whole man. Your mind picks up where the body has left off and stresses in dreaded anticipation of the next session. Your spirit is downcast by the seeming futility of it all while your soul is worn, searching for a way out. It hurts—body, mind, spirit, and soul. The pain is strangling me.

> *How do you respond when you see, for the first time, your best friend lying in the hospital, not knowing if she will live or die? I said to myself, "That's her body that's lying there, but how is she? How is her soul?" The problem with inward pain is sometimes it goes unnoticed and buried for years. It takes longer to heal. There is no way she could have made it without something taking place with her inwardly. I couldn't take away my friend's physical pain, but I could love away some of her mental pain just by being there when she needed me.*
>
> **—Lori Smith**, friend

The problem of pain is its potential. Pain has the capability to reach past the natural man and afflict the spiritual man or vice versa. Pain management is a crucial part of burn care for a burn survivor. Sometimes it's not the burn itself, nor the smoke inhalation, but just pain, all alone, that will cause your demise. The burn team must focus on controlling the physical pain you are experiencing because it is vital for your survival. Pain enhances your anxiety, and you cannot be happy and peaceful when it is prevailing.

Solomon, one of the wisest men ever to live, said in the book of Proverbs, "A merry heart doeth good like a medicine: but a broken spirit drieth the bones" (17:22). *Merry* is an intriguing word. What is a "merry heart"? It is indicative of being in high spirits, hopeful and in control. A merry heart is a heart that is optimistic and believes that everything will be all right. When we are able to take it a step further and just laugh, it can have a profound effect on our health.

If I were a doctor, after the burn patient had passed the threat of survival, I would prescribe a minimum of ten minutes of gut-wrenching laughter a day. The dosage of laughter would increase, according to the severity of the injury. Laughter stirs up the will to live. The flipside Solomon referred to is a broken spirit, a spirit that is destitute of hope, one that has given up. A broken spirit is one in which pessimism is the reality and the patient is waiting on the end. This type of brokenness dries the bones and strips away hope. Your emotional state is a crucial part of your recovery. What is happening on the inside directly affects what is happening on the outside.

> *The problem with pain is that our natural reflex is to avoid it at all costs. The very thought of it produces a nearly uncontrollable, visceral response to flee and withdraw. Over the years, we have managed, although not eliminated, my son's physical pain; however, the psychological pain has been a far greater challenge. A constant companion in one capacity or another, we have learned not to fear it but rather to live with it.*
> —**Lori Ferdock**, Douglassville, PA, mother of burn survivor

The pain was most difficult for me when I first woke from the coma. Before I could even focus well, I felt the assault. My whole body was throbbing as if a gang had beaten me all over with hammers. I hurt in places in my body that I didn't even know existed. It was a frightening experience. I didn't know what to think.

I have a fairly high pain tolerance, both physically and emotionally. By nature, I am an optimistic person. But in that moment, when my eyes popped open and I tumbled unarmed into the burn world, for a split second, I didn't see anything worth living for. Thank God for children and family who drew me back in from that morbid thought.

Another memorably painful time was when I woke up in the recovery room after a skin grafting surgery. Skin grafting is a process where skin is cut from an area that is not burned, known as a donor site. That skin is then stretched and put over the exposed area to replace the skin lost to a third-degree or above burn. I always felt an odd, burning sensation during that time. When I was a patient, the donor site was covered with scarlet red. After surgery, you would have to spend an allotted amount of time under a dry lamp to dry out the scarlet red so that it could eventually be pulled off. Peeling it off prematurely was akin to ripping your skin off without anesthesia.

Our family is known for having a high pain tolerance. However, having a high pain tolerance can be a curse. We were about two years out from the fire when one day I noticed Joseph wasn't running around as usual. Joseph, eight years old, was like an Energizer bunny. He did not stop. He was all over the place. Everything he did, he did fast.

I was reclining in the front room, really relaxed, when I called out to him, "Joseph, you okay?"

His reply was soft but strong: "Yes, ma'am."

Another fifteen minutes passed, and I still hadn't seen Joseph. I called out again, "Joe, everything all right?"

He replied the same way: "Yes, ma'am."

My relaxed demeanor was slowly fading. My motherly instincts kicked in double time, and I sat straight up. Jonathon came by as I did. I tried to be calm.

"Jonathon, what are you and Joe doing?"

"I'm trying to think of something to do. Joseph is in bed."

I was on my feet in an instant and at his bed within seconds. I knew Joseph. He would never be in bed in the middle of the day. He was way too inquisitive and hyper for that. There was one reason and one reason only that Joseph was lying down: he was sick. The mere fact that I had not seen him in motion for more than half an hour led me to believe that he had to be very sick at that.

Jonathon and Joseph shared a twin/full red, metal bunk bed set. Because of his fondness of heights and dream to become a pilot, Joseph always took the top bunk. I stepped on the bottom bed and peered over the top bunk, astonished at what I saw. There under the Barney comforter was a little, blue face. My voice was barely above a whisper.

"Can you breathe, Joseph?"

His reply was a soft, "No, ma'am."

I came undone. I knew he was having a severe asthma attack.

"Jonathon! Bring me the phone and hurry!"

I turned to Joseph and said, "When you can't breathe, baby, you are not okay."

He just stared at me and nodded yes.

Jonathon responded to the urgency in my voice.

I called 911. It happened that paramedics were leaving a call in the neighborhood right around the corner. They came and stabilized Joseph, and we were on our way to the emergency room. He had a two-week hospital stay from that episode.

I wanted to know why he didn't respond to the pain he had to be feeling. It hurts when you are laboring to breathe, and it's frightening. But he did respond—just not the way I thought he should have. I would have been frantic, running to my mother for help. Joseph chose to be still and quiet and to hope that it would pass.

A NOTE TO CAREGIVERS

This is an important lesson for caregivers and loved ones of burn survivors. Not everyone responds to pain the way you do. In fact, you can take several people with the same injuries and get several different responses to the pain. To one, it will hurt a little, while another person may be pulling his hair out. Caregivers gauge responses. The response your loved one gives is your cue for what to do or not to do; it is the compass you use to discern what direction to go in. The fault in that system lies in predetermining how a person should respond or in using your own pain threshold as the standard.

On the burn unit, there are no standard responses. You have to know something about the individual person in order to make a good judgment. Joseph's pain tolerance is on a level all by itself. I learned something about Joseph with his asthma attack that prepared me for another serious episode.

One day when Joseph was a sophomore in high school, the school nurse called. Just the fact that he was in the nurse's office had me lacing my shoe strings, preparing to get to him. The nurse was saying something about his stomach hurting and his not looking too well. I thanked her for calling and told her I was on my way.

Joseph looked slightly pale and was walking with a slight bend on his right side. I asked him how he was doing—I guess for the formality of it. He said he was hurting a little on his right side. He had admitted to the pain without prompting. I didn't have to ask if his side hurt. That was my cue to skip the pediatrician and head straight to the emergency room. I know that sounds dramatic, but years of observing my child had made me wise.

Of course, when we got to the ER, the nurse asked him, "On a scale of one to ten, what is your pain level?" I knew we were heading in the wrong direction with this question. I tried to intervene.

"Ma'am," I explained, "you cannot take what he says at face value. Please move him three or four faces towards ten when he responds."

She looked at me sympathetically.

"Everyone knows his own pain level. We have to take the patient's word for this. Sorry, Mom."

As true as those words were, they were not true for Joe.

Naturally, Joseph told them a two. By Joseph's standards, that was the average man's twenty. The nurse did just what I thought she would do. She took his vitals and set him in a corner until the more urgent patients were seen. Meanwhile, Joseph began to throw up violently and even let out a groan. I diagnosed Joseph myself and became more adamant about his being seen. To me, he had all the signs of a ruptured appendix. His pain just wasn't a ten according to that silly chart.

I pressed until he was finally taken to get an MRI of his stomach. They called in a surgeon to do an emergency operation to remove his appendix before it ruptured. I knew what was going on because I knew him. I knew that it is always best to help or sympathize with your loved one's pain according to what you know about him or her.

When I visit patients on the unit, I never assume they feel like I felt. I try to focus on what the individual is saying—as well as what he is not saying.

Nonverbal cues can be instructive. After two or three visits, I begin to get a feel for when a patient is hurting and needs to rest.

A NOTE TO BURN SURVIVORS

Have you ever been lying in your hospital bed during the critical stage of your injury, half dead, hurting so badly that you don't know what exactly is hurting? Then a well-meaning visitor, perhaps a family member or even a friend, approaches your door with a gigantic smile spread across his face and asks, "How are you doing?" It's a totally insane moment. Your response is guarded. You know if you say, "Good," he will be silly enough to believe you. And if you say, "Not so well," he will ask you an even more ridiculous question: "What's wrong?" You don't even know what's wrong!

I know what it feels like to be on the receiving end of absurd questions. I used to humor myself with a game I made up called RR, which stood for "Real Response." In this game, RRs were imaginary planes on suicide mission towards a visitor's head, equipped with the real message I wanted to give, exploding on contact. Yes, I have a vivid imagination.

Someone might walk in the room while the therapist was there, bending the living daylights out of my fingers, and ask me, "Does it hurt?" I then would imagine my RR with "Dummy" on it, flying over and hitting the visitor smack in the center of his forehead. By the way, questions like that, I didn't even bother to answer.

What I have come to understand is that people don't mean any harm; they often just don't know what to say. A word of advice to visitors: When you don't know what to say, talk about you or what's happening outside of the hospital. Don't just say anything to fill the space. Outside news is great to hear, especially when you have been confined on the burn unit for an extended period of time.

Distraction is a perfect tactic to help someone past his pain. I used this with my children many times over. I had a house full of active boys. Some bone was broken on somebody every week. The ER knew us by name. When we came in, they would say in a joking manner, "Hello, Mrs. Page, which son and what bone?" When I sat in the ER with the boys, I would get them to talking about anything and everything. I refused to sit and just stare at the source of pain. I knew the more my son looked at the injury, the worse he would feel.

The same is true for us. My advice to the patient is to steer your visitor's conversation in the direction you want it to go. When you don't feel like discussing *you*, redirect the conversation by asking questions about him.

My pastor's wife was a genius at this. Sister Jones always knew what to say or do in any situation, and in her wisdom, she also knew when to be quiet. It was an amazing thing to behold. She had a way about her that drew you to her, especially if you were hurting. It didn't matter how small or big the situation. She made you feel your problem was valid and took your feelings seriously.

Sister Jones was a major source of help and consolation during my turbulent times in the hospital. She could feel what I felt and hurt where I hurt. She would get right there with me, and together we would work it out. She was wise enough not to leave me out of the solution process. Her wisdom was like a salve for the soul. I will forever be grateful for her kindness.

There was only one thing I hated more than my daily tank visit: therapy. The therapists were terrorists in my eyes. Their mission was to torture, wreak havoc on the body, and destroy any semblance of sanity. Therapy was outright painful. At the end of every session, I swore to myself that it didn't matter if I used my hands again or walked; I wasn't going through that hell over and over again.

The face-off every day was tense. On a daily basis, I had to make a conscious decision to continue. My mind would scream, *Leave me alone!* But the therapists had power. They wooed me with that sympathetic smile and patient demeanor. I surrendered my rights every time. Then the torture started over again. I was medicated before and after every session. Vicodin and morphine were employed; it took powerful stuff. Yet, those drugs only managed to take the edge off. There was no way to escape the suffering fully. My option of choice to face the day was to endure. Endurance was my hero. Endurance had an influential ally called hope. Hope whispered the sweet promises of joy at the end. As long as I had hope, I could endure. The longer I endured, the more clearly I could see joy waiting for me. In essence, I countered my pain with endurance.

The back and buttocks are sensitive areas to be burned. My back was my most painful spot. I dreaded when it was time to remove the bandages. The pain would reverberate through every nerve in my body. The tank felt like a torture chamber. Then a constant discomfort would descend and continue until the pain meds kicked in. There was a tech on the unit who worked the night shift and had the perfect remedy for soothing my back when it was irritated and itchy: Crisco lard. I waited for her with just as much enthusiasm and joy as a child waits for the ice cream truck to come by. I knew that when she came in, she would spread that lard all over my back, and I would eventually get a good night's sleep. That may sound ridiculous to some of you, but it was real comfort for me. What is soothing to a person in pain is sometimes out of the box, whether it is physical or emotional pain.

Emotionally, I felt better when I was helping someone. I didn't care much about everyone doing everything for me. Don't get me wrong, I appreciated every single thing that was done to help. It was, however, therapeutic for me to be able to give something too—even if it was just hope or a kind word.

Out of the multitude of therapy sessions that I had, there were two sessions in particular that I remember vividly. The first was an outpatient visit that my sister-in-law had taken me to. My occupational therapist was a no-nonsense guy with clear objectives and a strategic plan to get results. When he said pick up twenty rubber bands, nineteen was a failure. He said what he meant and meant what he said. You could cry, complain, or scream—as long as the exercise was completed. He got the job done. My sister-in-law sat in a seat beside me, her eyes a pool of tears before the splint was even taken off. I slowly unwrapped the ace bandages and gingerly slipped the splint off. It fell on the table with a thud. Julia jumped.

"Sorry," she said nervously.

Michael gave her a stern glance as he took my hand and began examining it and massaging it. My palms were super sensitive, meaning every touch was exaggerated and an unpleasant experience. He began centering in on the scar bands and the first ripple of pain gripped me. I grimaced and Julia squirmed, placing her hand over her mouth to stop her outcry. Michael gave her a longer glance. The pain was intensifying as he moved from one hand to the other. I could not stop the tears.

Julia appeared to be in more severe pain than I was. I could hear her muffled sobs, but I refused to look at her.

"We can't have you here crying. Please leave if this upsets you," Michael said in an authoritative voice.

Julia apologized, wiped her eyes, and nodded her understanding. Then the torturous part began. Each finger had to be bent at every joint. The pain was excruciating. The tears and muffled whimpers came unbidden from Julia and me.

Michael stopped abruptly. When he said, "Get out," I felt as if he was the rudest person on earth. But he was right to do so. I was in enough pain all by myself. I did not need to compound and complicate my pain by adding hers.

I learned a valuable lesson from that therapy visit. Pain is contagious. When a friend or caregiver's emotional immune system is weak, he will catch your pain. If your resistance is low, you will catch his pain. You wind up swapping "pain germs." It was not Julia's intention to do so, but her discomfort was escalating mine. When you are in severe pain, it is not a good time to take on the burden of another person's pain. It took courage to guard against that.

The other visit was also an outpatient visit. My pastor's wife, Sister Jones, was with me at this appointment. She sat beside me and quietly watched as Michael went through the same routine. Occasionally, she would give me a compassionate smile. Her demeanor suggested that she understood how tough this was for me and that she was willing to do anything to help. I was encouraged to be brave.

Michael smiled at her occasionally. "Justina is a tough lady, isn't she?" he said as he worked with the digits on the left hand.

"Yes, she is," Sister Jones said, smiling.

We then shared a smile between ourselves, both of us understanding the deeper implications of what the therapist had said. As the session went on, Sister Jones called her husband and asked him to pray for me. Tears were falling down her face.

For a space, I had the impulse to pray for her. I was momentarily distracted from my own pain. Her action was a candid display of compassion that moved me greatly. I felt undergirded. She was transferring strength and allowing a space for me to dump some of my pain. It was the best session I ever had. I learned yet another lesson. Pain can be eased by compassion, understanding, or strength.

As annoying as it is, pain has a purpose. Pain is our internal siren that alerts us that something is wrong. Life without pain is a life that can be cut short prematurely. Think about it. Our major diseases and health risks are diagnosed because pain drove us to the hospital to get our bodies examined.

Pain tells us something is happening that needs to be fixed. Can you imagine having stomach cancer and feeling no discomfort or pain? The cancer would eat you alive. Pain has birthed some of the greatest blessings I have in my life; it was pain that brought forth my six precious sons.

When I was weight training during basketball season, pain was the indicator that let me know I was getting stronger. When you are on a weightlifting regimen, pain lets you know you are getting a good workout and strengthening your muscles. Emotional pain can have a similar effect.

People who experience emotional pain have an opportunity to become stronger in many areas as well. My compassion is much greater now. I try harder to hear what people are saying, rather than trying to make sure they understand me. Even though it is next to impossible to live this life without experiencing some form of pain, we do have consolation. Pain can be managed, soothed, and healed. We can then draw wisdom from our experiences with pain to help those who are standing in shoes we ourselves have worn.

Left: Enjoying the river walk in San Antonio

Prayer

Heavenly Father, I come to you in the name of Jesus.

I am hurting. Please help me with the pain.

I don't know what to do. Can you take it away?

My back and my hands are so sore.

Sometimes I cannot think for the pain.

My heart is hurting also. The hurt is deep.

You told us to cast our cares on you because you care for us.

Do you see what I am going through? I thank you for Jesus, our High Priest,

who is touched with the feelings of our infirmities.

Please help me to hold on.

In Jesus' name I pray.

Amen.

Chapter 9

DEPTHS OF DESPAIR

Life is no longer good or peaceful.
Life is infested with pain, sorrow, and despair.

I am nothing. I am scarred from head to toe. I have nothing. I don't even own the clothes on my back. I can't do anything. I need someone to assist me with menial tasks. I want to fast forward to the end that I am sure is coming. Life is no longer good or peaceful. Life is infested with pain, sorrow, and despair.

What is the use in hanging on? Hope has fled, and courage has hidden itself. Pain is the present tyrant; sorrow and despair are the reigning princes. I no longer care what happens. The fight is gone. I am weary from fear and in need of peace.

Those were my thoughts three days after I awoke from the coma. Even being surrounded with the best support system in the world and being lifted up by daily encouragement, I fell into despair. I would love to say I knew I was going to make it from the beginning, but that would be dishonest. I did not commune with despair long, but the short courtship we had was terrifying. It is simply awful to feel like you are on a sinking ship and there is nothing anyone can do.

Lying in that bed, in a mask of tubes and needles, unable to move, I was shrouded in a blanket of hopelessness. I never felt closer to death's door in all my life. It was as if one foot had already crossed the threshold and time was going to help the other foot over.

Everyone was trying to encourage me. No visitors came with an openly evil intent. Even those who were slightly discouraging meant no harm. Their hearts were in the right place; they just lacked wisdom. At that point in my life, the point of deepest despair, it was up to me to make the decision to overcome my circumstance or not. Others could help me, but I could make it out *only* if and when I decided I wanted it.

Despair will place you in solitary confinement. You can't see anyone, talk to anyone, or be allowed to see natural daylight. Your only nourishment is the junk it brings you.

I abhor violence, but I am an advocate of self-defense. I feel we have a right to protect ourselves by any means necessary. Despair dominates when we waive our right to protect ourselves. We do this by giving up and deciding not to fight.

Despair is not fair. It will not stop punching when you stop; it will keep throwing blows until you are knocked out. Despair is an unprincipled enemy.

I am an analytical thinker, and in principle, fighting in other contexts never made much sense to me. My observations in life had revealed some disconcerting things regarding fights. First of all, I noticed that more often than not, the people fighting had no idea what they were fighting about. Second, they usually started off as friends. Third, and most annoying to me, was the way that the people who instigated the whole mess would watch from the outside, egging it on.

Even with my distaste for fights, I found myself always fighting. Why? I rarely fought for myself; all but two of my slew of fights were for others. I was a protector. I hated seeing people being taken advantage of. If they couldn't protect themselves, I felt obligated to help. My point is this: Many people come to a place where a fight is necessary. Despair is one of those places. You have to fight until you win. Sometimes other burn survivors have to jump in with their wisdom and experience to help.

One day, a week or so after I awoke from the coma, I noticed that my nurse was visiting my room more frequently than usual. My thoughts had been sabotaged by fear, and despair had paralyzed me. All I could think of was making sure I had peace with God. I had given up trying to figure out if the boys and my husband would be all right. There was nothing that I could do anyway.

As the morning went on, my fear and despair escalated. I felt myself entering a mental tunnel of dread and doom. I knew this was *the* day. I could feel it with every fiber of my being; this was the day I would pass on and leave this side of life. The sound of the breathing machine confirmed my feelings. The steady, rhythmic beep I had grown accustomed to hearing was now an erratic thump of different pitches and sounds. I assumed the audible beeping rhythm was my heartbeat. I'm dying, I thought, and no one is here to see.

Where was my husband? I was on my deathbed, and he wasn't even there in my final hour. My sorrow and self-pity doubled. I felt he of all people should have been there beside me in my dying hour. I would have called for him if I could, but I had been robbed of all forms of communication except my eyes. The nurse could not read them. He smiled when we made eye contact, but he was oblivious to my trepidation. It was vexing.

The beeps were longer now. I began to look for the light. I had always heard the testimonies of Christians who had near death experiences; each survivor said he saw a bright light, Jesus coming to get him. I didn't see the light. Had I forgotten to repent about something? Beep, beep, beep, beeeep . . . Oh, God help me . . . beeep, beep, beep, beeeeep . . . Jesus…beeep, beep, beeeeep, beeeeep . . . Where is my husband? I love you . . . beeeeeeeep, beeeeeeeep.

I closed my eyes. It was over for real . . . beeeeeeeep . . . then silence. My heart has stopped. I am dead.

My eyes flew open at the nurse's touch on my shoulder. I was hoping for the archangel Michael. I had never been so glad to see another human being in my life.

"Mrs. Page, I am sorry to wake you."

Of course I was not asleep; I was dead or about to die—or so I thought.

"You are breathing pretty well on your own. We are going to remove the breathing tube from your throat as soon as Dr. Freet gets back on the unit."

The rest of the nurse's message fell on deaf ears. What? The beep that terrified me was the machine shutting down—not my heart. Despair had painted a picture of death while God was working a miracle. I was dumbfounded.

It was a grueling task, but the tube was removed no longer than fifteen minutes after the nurse spoke with me, and I never needed it again. As the nurse put ice chips on my lips, I tried my best to hold back the hysterical laughter whirling in my belly. I lost the battle. The irony of it all got the best of me. The tears and laughter mingled quite comfortably. I couldn't even gather my composure to explain myself.

The nurse politely excused himself—I'm sure to check my charts for mental instability. I didn't care. For the first time since I had been in the hospital, I felt a seed of hope, real hope, a powerful defense against despair. It was the last tussle I lost with despair. Was I ever tempted by despair again? Of course, but it never ever sat in the driver's seat again.

Despair takes hold when your pain and problems are at the forefront and in clear focus. Despair takes root when solutions elude you. The depth of despair is a downward spiral into nothingness. The end product of despair is emotional and/or physical death. Despair paints a deceptive picture. It displays false things as true and makes true things look impossible to overcome. It is the perfect platform for defeat. Despair is a common response to a turbulent experience. It is nothing to be ashamed of or to hide.

The experience with the breathing tube made me decide never to fall into that psychological pit again. I hated the place that despair took me in my short acquaintance with it.

When fighting for your life and sanity, you have to use every available tool within reach. Hatred was only an arm's length away. Therefore, my hatred became a useful resource. I hated with a passion what had happened to my family. I hated that my children were robbed of their innocence and safety at such an early age. I hated that I had dealt with self-esteem issues for the majority of my life and now this. Most of all, I hated losing Amos. My hatred needed a safe outlet, a punching bag to tear into, that it might not destroy me or others. Despair became the target. I used hatred to cross swords with despair.

I began to break my fall into despair through H.A.T.R.E.D, an acronym for my personal six-step method that I practiced when despair raised its ugly head.

H stands for hope. From that point on, I was determined to hope at all times. It didn't matter if it was for five things or one thing. It didn't matter if it was hope for life or grape juice the next morning. It really doesn't matter what you hope for at all—just hope. Hope keeps you fighting. Fighting keeps you living. Living gives you time, and time has the power eventually to bring you to the place you desire to be. Hope sends a signal to your brain that says, *No matter the circumstance, it is my intention to live.* A hopeful mindset breaks through barriers that would otherwise imprison you. If I continued to see myself lying in the bed and never getting up, I would more than likely be lying in bed today. Hope gave me an incentive to act. My hope is still alive today. No matter what I accomplish, I set my eye on a greater hope. It is a rewarding process.

A stands for ask. Ask for help when you are struggling. It is hard to admit that you are struggling with despair, especially when you are known for your faith. When despair is attacking, it is not the time for a one-man show. Despair fights dirty and aims below the belt. It is not cowardly to get back up in that fight—especially in a fight for your life. Asking for help was not my strong suit. If it is at all possible, I like to do everything myself. That attitude has both a good side and a bad side. For a long period of time, my pride would not let me disclose my doubts, pain, and fear. I wanted everyone to be all right. I didn't want others' faith to waiver because of my seeming lack of faith. But reality has a way of rushing in on the shores of our life. Like an unexpected wave surge on the shores of a sandy beach, reality rushes in and knocks down all of the artificial sand castles we build when trying to appear strong and faithful. Asking for help grounds you and reveals a powerful truth about you: you are human.

T means think again. Despair is a mind battle. Combat discouraging thoughts with a counter thought. You may have been told that there was a 50 percent chance that your right hand would have to be amputated. Thinking about that statement alone can be devastating. However, the counter thought is that there is a 50 percent chance that it will not have to be amputated.

When despair grips you, how you think is half the battle. This is true because actions follow thoughts. More importantly, even if no one else does, you will believe your own thoughts. Thinking again is like a seesaw ride. Despair sits on a seat and says, "You might die." You have to sit on the other seat and swing the lever back down and say, "I might live." Despair might say, "You will lose an arm." You have to think again and say, "I still have one arm." The perspective you take will aid your success.

R stands for reason. You have a reason to live. It could be children, a spouse, or a purpose. Purpose is powerful, especially when you are determined to fulfill it. Hope is supported by your reason. Your reason could simply be because you want to.

When the boys were younger, my husband and I would let them choose their own movie at Blockbuster. One particular evening, Jonathon was really outraged with Joseph. There was a three-part series to one of the new cartoons, and he and Caleb had unsuccessfully tried to convince Joseph to get the third part. Joseph did not budge.

"Joseph, we need part three," Jonathon said in an irritated tone. "You always get plane movies. What is your reason for getting another plane movie?"

Joseph answered him in a calm voice, "Because I want to. It is my choice." Pretty profound for a six-year-old.

When you are assaulted by despair, you may not have the typical reasons to fight like some people. But a reason still exists: do it because you want to. It's your choice.

E means expose your emotions. Not just to anyone, though. Choose a person you trust, one who is available to be a sounding board for you. I suggest you pick someone

Blockbuster time for Caleb, Jonathon, & Joseph

with wisdom, who is stable and willing to go the distance with you. Your most destructive fungi and bacteria breed in the dark. Hiding anxiety multiplies your trepidation.

One thing I've learned to do after much failing and heartache is to be honest and upfront. If I'm angry, I'm angry. If I'm scared, I'm scared. If you were on a cruise ship heading to the Bahamas and the ship sprang a serious leak, you wouldn't sit there quietly in your cabin and sink. Once the waters began to rise in the boat and you understood the peril you were facing, you would cry out to someone for help, be it the captain or a friend. You would not feel one ounce of shame. And no one could blame you since your life was at stake.

The stakes are just as high and higher when despair grabs you during a traumatic situation. You do not need to be ashamed of the reason for nor the content of your despair. Let someone know where you are. What scares us most is that someone will find out how we feel. No one wants the stigma of being a coward. We fear that someone will discover that we are not as strong as we appear to be.

Where we appear to be emotionally can be a very different place from where we actually are. Admit where you are so you can get to a healthier state, to where you want to be. Exposing despair gives you better leverage to do that and puts you in a position to get help from others.

D stands for demanding thankfulness from yourself. After some time had passed, I began counting my blessings every morning. There is always so much to be thankful for. When you find yourself at the end of a particularly grueling day, one in which nothing went right, relapses into gloom are imminent. When you feel the pain taking you to the edge, try to be grateful for the one thing that is left: life. Life means another chance. Perhaps the next day will be better.

Failing to be thankful has resulted in a major downfall for many people. We take for granted so many things, failing to appreciate every gift, person, and opportunity we are afforded. I made it a practice to count my blessings every day. I had time to do that in the morning before any visitors came. The things that I allowed myself to be thankful for became a stairwell out of the depths of despair. The more I counted, the higher I climbed. I would start with what some may call the simple things.

Grape juice is on my tray this morning, and I love grape juice. God, I thank you for the lady who brought the grape juice. When I had my shower today, I noticed that my back didn't hurt as bad. God, I thank you for the tech who has been so gentle. Eventually, I would work my way up to the big three: life, family, and friends. I do understand that some patients lose both family and friends.

There are still two major things every person who is reading this book has left: life and opportunity. The marriage of the two is where the power is. Opportunity without life is vain; there is nothing that comes from that. Life lived without taking advantage of opportunity is painful and will keep you in the same spot for an eternity. But when we recognize and esteem the life we have and let opportunity have a free-for-all in our lives, the rewards will be staggering.

My earliest memory of despair happened when I was eight years old. My mother and my four siblings and I were living in Los Angeles, California. I was a timid and shy child in my early years. I was much taller than all of my classmates, had short hair, and was as skinny as a bean pole. My self-esteem was shot. It didn't help that both of my sisters were beauties—at least in my eyes.

On the first day of school in a new city with a brand new class, I was confronted on the playground by the third grade school bully. Vickie had a firm understanding with all the class: do what I say. Everyone obliged her. Vickie wanted my lunch that day. I felt I had no choice but to give it to her. My mother would make the best lunches in the world. She was creative, and we wouldn't know what surprise to expect from her.

I told my sister Kelly about it on the way home. Kelly was not even five feet at that time, but was tough as nails. She probably was the fifth grade bully. I'm not sure, but I depended on her for protection. Kelly's reprimand surprised me. She told me that if Vickie could take my lunch, she would take my snack herself—until I stood up and fought back. A few days passed and Vickie was taking my lunch daily as Kelly took my snack. That Thursday, I finally told my mother. I was in for an even more devastating surprise. My mother said, "If Vickie can take your lunch and Kelly can take your snack, then Kelly could also take your dinner. Don't give Vickie your lunch."

Despair descended on me like a thunderstorm. I felt trapped. As it appeared, no one was on my side. In my eight-year-old eyes, everyone had forsaken me. Vickie had been taking lunches from whomever she willed for the past two years. In a third grader's mind, that was forever. I didn't know what I was going to do. I wept all night long. Friday morning, I woke up, with eyes swollen from crying and feeling the impending dread of the day. Of all days, it seemed as if my mother purposely packed the best lunch in the world with all my favorite things, including sliced peaches. On the way to school that day, the tears came unwillingly. Kelly would glance over at me every now and then.

Finally, she said, "Stop crying. All you have to do is tell her no. Stand up for yourself and fight."

Her words did little to comfort me. We were on the playground again when Vickie sauntered over with a devious grin on her face and demanded I hand over the lunch. I tried to bargain with her. I offered everything but my peaches. I really wanted my peaches. She laughed, and her three supporters joined in. She took a step closer to me and her smile faded.

"I want the lunch. All of it."

Before I knew it, "No," had flown out of my mouth. She was shocked. It took her a few seconds to recover.

Then she said, "I guess I will just have to take it."

My grip tightened on the brown bag in my hand. I tried to plead with her.

"Please, Vickie, I don't want to fight."

She mocked me, repeating my words and laughing. Then she made a terrible mistake; she reached for me. The next thing I remember, the police were pulling me off of her. I didn't succumb to despair or allow her to take my lunch that day because there was something I wanted badly. I wanted my peaches.

Despair is a ruthless enemy to trauma recovery. But it is not an invincible foe. The picture despair paints is a half reality. Let's take the brush of hope and finish the picture. We can tap into the faith, hope, and love that resides deep down inside of us to overcome just about anything.

Prayer

Heavenly Father, I come to you in the name of Jesus.

I know you are real, but it doesn't seem to matter right now.

I feel so low, lower than I have ever felt in my life. Is this my end?

Will I die like this? Nothing is right anymore.

All I can see is pain and suffering.

I have never felt this way before.

Please help me. I know you are stronger than what I am feeling right now.

I know my soul should not be so downcast. I will put my trust in you.

You are the lifter of my countenance.

In Jesus' name I pray,

Amen.

Chapter 10

FAITH CRISIS

*Gone was the completeness I once
was united with. Where was God?*

O n Mother's Day, May 11, 1997, God had blessed me with fraternal twins, Amos Beniah and Benjamin Josiah. My quiver was full and complete, and I could not have been prouder. I imagined glimpses of the twins' future, growing up together and wearing matching outfits. I envisioned one singing while the other is preaching; one batting while the other is pitching—but never one living and the other dying.

I had no idea that in just twenty-two short months, I would be facing the devastating emotional pain inflicted by this altered pattern to their lives. The sorrow of losing one son and the narrow escape of the other twin cast the dreaded shroud of doubt and fear over me. I found myself a year after the fire, on May

11, 2000, facing an emotional battle. How could I rejoice in the survival of one twin while mourning the death of the other?

I resolved this confusing dilemma through many tears and much prayer. I came to the conclusion that Benjamin should not be denied the celebration due him on his birthday. He was a survivor after all. He had overcome a ton of obstacles and that in itself was worth giving God thanks for.

So every May 11, I celebrate Ben and the odds he surmounted. On May 10, sometime in the evening hours, I mourn Amos and the devastating loss of not having him with us. Sometimes I just try to remember as much as I can about his likes and dislikes, his favorite foods, his favorite things to do. Sometimes I just cry.

In the beginning, it was difficult. When Benjamin would pull his trachea tube out, it was as if he was trying to hasten his death and reunite with his twin brother. Those were dreadful, fearful times, direct attacks on my faith. The enemy of my faith was fear. Fear opened a door for my faith to work in reverse, pushing me to anticipate every possible negative outcome. Gone was the completeness I once was united with. Where was God?

I have a habit of thinking about things over and over and over again, long after most people have forgotten about the matter at hand. Then I analyze and reanalyze, trying to put sense with actions and weed out a purpose.

I have a vivid memory of sitting on our porch alone when I was five years old, thinking about fathers. I had my left thumb across my lips and my other little fat fingers on my neck, a posture I still assume when I am deep in thought. I was leaning on my knees, which were pressed close to my chest, as I absently tapped the cement porch with my right hand. I grew up in a home without a father, and I was trying to figure out why some children had fathers and some children didn't.

I decided that I had to have one somewhere. I wanted to know who my father was and where he was. What was he doing? Why wasn't he with me? My thoughts began to plunge deeper. Maybe the good girls had fathers and the bad girls didn't. I let that thought rumble around in my little head for a while. I knew

I had been bad at times. I tried not to be bad all the time, but I had made many mistakes. I thought about my friends who didn't have fathers. Yep, they were bad sometimes too.

Then I thought about my friends with fathers. I jumped clear over the fact that they could be just as naughty as I was and focused on the positive things they did, how they shared or were nice to me. I never considered that I was nice and shared with them also. As crazy as it sounds, I felt as if I was getting somewhere. So, I reasoned, I didn't have my father around because I was a bad girl. That realization felt awful.

Another question sprang to mind. What if I started being good from that moment on—will he come then? That was a tough question for me. I had set up a deal in my mind. Be good, and then you can meet your father. Those were tough and unfair conditions. All the weight was on one side: mine. My father didn't have to do anything, just come home.

I was mighty afraid I couldn't hold up my end of the bargain. The more I thought about it, the more depressed I got. I knew I was going to make another mistake. So I just gave up. I wouldn't have a father and that was that. As I stood and straightened out my rumpled shorts, my last thoughts were those of futility. Forget having a father—who needs him, anyway?

After the fire, I found myself having the same, warped, five-year-old thought pattern. Why was I the one who got burned? Was it because God was not pleased with me? I never considered that the other ten patients on the unit were probably asking the same question. If my family could wake up to an inferno, lose a child, and suffer the injuries we had, anything could happen.

My heavenly Father had left, obviously because I was bad. Something was wrong. God had forsaken me.

Thank God for spiritual fathers. The first words my pastor said to me when I awoke from the coma was, "This is not your fault. God is not judging you. You haven't done anything wrong." I really needed to hear that. I was accustomed to my pastor telling me truth whether it was convenient or not. Because of his frankness, it was no problem to believe him; I knew he wouldn't say just anything.

After I settled it in my mind that it wasn't my fault, I wanted to find out the answer to the big question: why?

When you are trudging through a faith crisis, your mind is bombarded with tough, incriminating questions. You are pressed with questions with an implied answer in mind. Why didn't you put batteries in the smoke detector? The implied answer is, I should have. How could you not get Amos out? The implied answer is, I didn't. What are you going to do now? The implied answer is, it's over. Where is your God? Again, the implied answer is, he left me.

When I was faced with these and many other implicating questions, it helped me when I rehearsed the charges to a friend. At the onset of my tragedy, I was wounded, hurt, depressed, afraid, and angry. At the same time, I was reaching for my faith. My emotions were all over the place. I was not in a good place mentally to think through those questions clearly.

I needed someone spiritual to help me think rationally.

The natural course of life is for children to bury their parents. When that pattern is reversed, the shock and grief are intensified and the fear escalates. The fruit of faith is contentment, patience, and strength. The fertilizer of my faith was my family. I had given up everything, making many sacrifices to ensure the stability of the family. When the seed of fear took root, that fruit was tarnished. The disruption blindsided me and crippled my faith in the process. In the garden of my heart, the weeds of bitterness, fear, and most potent, unforgiveness had taken root.

Faith and fear are not compatible roommates. They do not work together. They pull in opposing directions, and one will always dominate the other. Friends counted on my faith. Many people leaned on me for support and encouragement. Even in my hospital bed at my weakest point, people came to confide in me and draw strength from me.

The dilemma was bewildering. Who could I talk to? Who would understand the intensity of the faith crisis I was in? Only God.

God lost a son, his only son, to an unjust death on the cross. It was a tragic loss, yet a loss with purpose. Salvation is now available for people all over the world. Ironically, it is available to people who may or may not accept him. I asked God to forgive me and for strength to forgive the landlord who did not make sure the wiring was in code.

"Show me," I said, "how you dealt with the loss of your Son."

The scriptures stir my spirit: "For God so loved the world that he gave his only begotten Son" (John 3:16).

"All things work together for good to them that love God" (Rom. 8:28). But God, even this? I cannot sit, stand, walk, or use my hands. I am totally dependent. My son has facial burns and is now mentally retarded. My other sons are traumatized. My husband is wearing a cloak of failure. I hurt physically; I hurt emotionally. One son is hurt; another is dead."

God answers me; he is not afraid of my true emotions. "My son died, yet he rose and lives again. Your son also lives," he says. I am challenged. I had accepted Christ many years earlier and believed in the hope of eternal life.

Now my son had slipped into that eternal place where I had prayed for him to be one day since his birth. I chose to embrace my faith and not abandon it. God had saved Amos. God had lent him to me for a season, and now he had taken him back. This was God's choice. I realized that in my relationship with God, I hadn't considered his choices. My desires had been the ruling authority.

Faith was not a major focus in my upbringing. My faith walk began on a college campus in Rolla, Missouri. I did not go to Rolla on a faith quest. My decision to go there was a product of pure stubbornness. I had narrowed my choices down to two campuses: the University of Kansas, the KU Jayhawks, and University of Missouri at Rolla, UMR. KU had an awesome ladies basketball team at that time, and I had already spent a summer semester there accumulating credits prior to my high school graduation. Rolla, my second choice, appealed to me only because of the difficulty it took to get accepted and the fact that my best friend wanted to go there.

I asked my trigonometry teacher for a recommendation letter for UMR. Another teacher, who had never had me in any of her classes, overheard my request and laughed. I asked her what was funny.

"Are you serious? You have to be the cream of the crop to get into that school."

That was a horrible thing for her to say, but she did have reason to think I was not so bright. I was not the class clown but the school clown.

The teachers who didn't have me in their classes thought I was a complete fool. Those who had the misfortune of having me in class knew I was a smart fool.

So what did I do? I got mad, gave her a few choice words, tore up my application to KU, and decided that UMR was the only place I would go. And there, at UMR, is where I made the decision to accept Jesus as my Lord and Savior.

This new birth was a major transformation for me. Now I had a father figure in my life for the first time, someone I could believe in. I had a protector, a provider, a guide, and someone to set boundaries. God was a problem solver and wonderful example. He was a constant—someone I could depend on. Most of my life, I had depended on me. Now I had someone I could trust, a heavenly Father, someone strong. I was curious about God's power. I wanted to know intimately the God who created mankind and parted the seas. I wanted to experience an extraordinary God.

Well, an extraordinary God needs extraordinary circumstances to manifest himself. The fire was the ideal stage for God to make an appearance:

Setting: A fire, in which a son is lost, a home destroyed, and family members are seriously burned
Time: March 7, 1999
Conflict: What now? How do we get back to normalcy? Where is God?
Protagonists: Page family
Antagonists: fear, anger, guilt, and pain
Deus ex machina: God
Resolution: God is a present help in the time of trouble.

Not long after I gave my life to Christ, I was reading my Bible and stumbled across a scripture that said, "If you ask anything in my name you will receive it" (). That was so exciting to me! I had a father who—I supposed—just did whatever I said. I believed that scripture with all my heart. This whole faith thing was new, exciting, and extraordinary.

I called my friend Sheila from my dorm room, willing her to pick up instantly. When she answered, I didn't even say hello.

"God told me he would give me my driver's license today!" I blurted out, half out of excitement and half anticipation. There was a moment of silence.

"What?" she said, obviously thinking I had lost my mind.

I became more animated.

"God said he would give me my driver's license today."

"Really?" That was all she could manage to say.

I was a babe in Christ. She was wisely being gentle with me.

"Yes. He said if I ask anything in his name, I can have it. I want my driver's license, so I can have it."

She didn't try to explain the scripture or reprimand me for my ridiculous thinking. She simply asked me a logical and wise question: "Can you drive?"

A short silence fell over the phone. I thought about what I could do, measured against what he said he could do. My faith kept speaking.

"Not very well. But a promise is a promise. God said I could have it."

I'm sure she didn't know what to say to me. I admit; I was a true piece of work. She offered a compromise.

"Why don't I come over and take you for a test drive first, so we can make sure you are ready for the test."

"If you think we need to practice first, that's fine. But I believe God will do what he says."

As she promised, Sheila picked me up in her grey Buick sedan. I got in the car, took the wheel, and drove absolutely horribly. I could not drive. Before we went inside the Department of Public Service office, she gave me a stern look and asked, "You sure you want to take this test, that God told you he was going to give you your license?"

I nodded my head yes. Her face was shadowed with doubt, but she simply said okay.

The test instructor was a tall, thin, elderly man who looked to be in his late sixties. He got in the car, rattled off some instructions, and we were on our way. I almost hit a tree, ran into someone's yard, and scared the poor man half to death. Still, I believed that I would get that driver's license.

I drove up to the DPS building. He pulled out his clipboard and added up my score. A look of shock overtook his face when he finished grading the test the first time. Then he did it over again, and again a third time. He looked over at me with wide eyes.

"Ma'am, I don't know how, but you passed this test."

I was elated. God had done what he said he would do. I ran to the car where Sheila was sitting, screaming, "I passed my test. Can I drive?"

Sheila's answer was a quick no. "I don't know what happened in there, but you don't know how to drive."

That was more than twenty-five years ago, and we still laugh about that incident. My faith was free and knew no boundaries.

Weeks after the fire, my faith collapsed into solitary confinement. I was only confident and sure about one thing: God is. I had to build my faith back up. I discovered that I didn't know God as I thought I did. I also came to the realization that God was not my genie; he did not move according to my command. Collapses happen when the structure of an unstable building is tampered with. That principle holds true when it comes to faith. Your faith is likely to collapse under the complexity and immense pressure of a tragic fire.

Patience is the sweet darling that faith is enamored with. Faith wouldn't be itself without it. The one thing we need if we are to avoid the quicksand that trials plummet us toward is patience.

Patience, simply put, is the ability to wait. Who wants to do that? That is a taboo in our society. Every bit of modern technology is designed to fulfill our whims faster. The more quickly the product works, the better it sells. Progress, we like to call it. This progress has unfortunately produced a general mentality that we should not have to wait for anything. It is embarrassing to think about how irritated I become when my computer takes fifteen seconds to boot up instead of five. What is that?

Even more disturbing is the image of me getting annoyed at the microwave because my burger needs a full minute to reheat and was not heated all the way through in forty-five seconds. We are spoiled.

It's not hard to compare this microwave mentality to our impatience as we wait for God's timing to come to pass. Many things for which we pray, we will receive through our faith. But time has a hand in everything. We cannot get around it.

When I first awoke from the coma, one of my first prayers was, "Lord, what is going on? Please fix the pain!" When I woke up the next morning hurting, I prayed the same prayer again. Every day, I prayer the same prayer.

Then weeks turned into months. Did I feel as if God did not hear me? Yes. But, time needed space to work. While time was doing its thing, I had to let patience do hers. When everyone was finished, the pain was managed.

> *From burn victim to burn survivor, from loss to wisdom, from grief to peace, Justina knows the journey. Each step of the way, she bore the insurmountable with a presence of grace and dignity, confident in her faith and family. The journey is not over for this remarkably inspiring woman. Her family's story is a rich blessing and a lesson in how to turn tragedy into an opportunity to make a difference.*
> –**Vina Drennan**, Common Voices Advocate; lost her husband, FDNY Captain John Drennan, from burns sustained while fighting a fire in 1994

One of the worst things you can do when you find yourself in a faith crisis is to stop praying. If you never prayed, it's a good time to start. If you stop praying, you lose communication. If you lose communication, you forfeit direction and encouragement. When you lose direction and encouragement, you are headed for a downward spiral.

Prayer is simply a conversation with God. Make sure that you keep that conversation honest. It can be brief. On many occasions, I have prayed one word: help.

Remember too that it is a conversation in which two people are talking: you and God. Sometimes you have to listen, and when you do hear, be willing to change.

What worked best for me was staying in fellowship with those of like faith. There is a tendency to want to withdraw and not want to be around people at all.

Fight that temptation. Even if it is just one or two people, keep yourself in good company. In good company is wise counsel that can help you along the way.

At the onset of a faith crisis, you begin to question what you have believed and trusted. It is a time when the bridge of faith, used to get from a difficult predicament to steady ground, looks unsteady and is scary to travel on.

Most people have doubts, fears, and questions every once in a while. During a crisis is when you need your faith the most, but you may trust it the least. It is a state of panic we fall into during uncertain times.

Panic is an emotion we experience in the presence of a threat. It's that automatic switch that flips on when danger jumps out of nowhere, catching us off guard, but it's a normal response. Panic has a dangerous side because you lose your ability to think and reason through a situation.

I panicked big time when I first woke up from the coma. Even though my body was confined to the bed, my mind was doing continual hundred-meter dashes. I was wearing myself out. Tragedy can lead you into a faith panic attack easily. A faith panic attack usually begins with two words: "I thought." *I thought God was watching over me. I thought we were Christians. I thought I was faithful. I thought God loved me.* You begin to question things you already have answers to.

Apart from this traumatic experience, I knew the answers. Yes, God was watching over me; of course, I am a Christian. I have striven to be faithful, and of course, God loves me. However, in the middle of my panic, those answers eluded me.

Most people have probably seen the Staples commercial in which the employees of various companies have access to a giant, red button called the "easy" button. In the midst of difficult situations, the employee just presses the magic "easy button," and his problems are solved instantaneously.

I can visualize a similar button for those of us who have been in or are currently in a faith crisis. We want a button that, upon pushing it, would completely take away the faith crisis. I would call it the "why" button. Pushing it could answer my questions and solve my problems: *Why did this happen? Why am I hurting? Why is my child gone? Why, why, why, why, why?* The problem is, when I am told why, what am I going to do then? The answers were likely to make me more upset.

Knowing why won't change anything that has already taken place. It's okay not to know why. Use your energy to seek answers to the questions that are going to get you somewhere: *How am I going to keep this from happening again? How do I handle the hurt? How do I deal with the death of my child?* Those questions point to the conundrum that, when answered, will get your faith moving again.

Among the many results of guilt, here are two: you will either deny the reality of how you feel in order to appear to be doing well, or you will cave under the pressure and give up altogether. Both scenarios are disastrous for you.

The strength you have is what you have, and the faith you have is your reality. Build on what you have. Don't compare yourself with anyone. They are not the standard. That is a tragic mistake. Faith is not to be compared, but to be experienced and grown. Sometimes we can look at the faith of others and feel ashamed.

You could be devastated because of a scar on your neck. It doesn't matter if Joe lost his leg and he is still able to smile. There is always more to the story. Maybe your scar has cost you your modeling career. Maybe Joe had diabetes and was mentally prepared for an amputation. Whatever the case, you have to deal with where *your* faith rests.

I came to a low place where all I had to hold on to was "God is." I held on to that truth as if my life depended on it. Of course, I knew a lot of other things theoretically, but the trauma had caused most of what I knew to become fuzzy. I took that simple knowledge, the assurance that God is, and began to add to my faith two other truths: God loves; God cares. Eventually, I got to a major building block: God can. If there is any faith left, no matter how small, you can grow it to the place you desire it to be, especially when it is authentic.

Tea with the Cottonballs –
Amos House of Faith volunteers

Prayer

Heavenly Father, I come to you in the name of Jesus.

I don't understand. Are you there? Can you hear me?

Why didn't you protect us from that fire? Where were you?

I have always trusted you. I don't even know what to believe.

Did I do something wrong? I am sort of confused.

I do know that you are God. The witness is inside of me.

I know I am bombarding you with whys. Help me to understand.

Show me how to get through these trials.

Please help me. I feel my faith crumbling.

Forgive me, and please don't be angry with me.

In Jesus' name,

Amen.

Chapter 11

GUILT

*Maybe instead of saving me twice,
there would have been time to save Amos.*

L ate at night, as I lay in my bed, agonizing, itching, and fidgeting, my
mind runs through one scenario after another. "What ifs" are assaulting
me, driving me, robbing me of my peace: *What if I had stayed outside
when my husband got me out the first time? Maybe instead of saving me twice, there
would have been time to save Amos. I wouldn't have been burned as badly, and I
could have been a help instead of a burden. What if we had bought the new house
and not waited for the perfect house—because I was so picky? Surely we would have
escaped the turmoil of this tragedy.*

The spirals of "what ifs" continued downward and dragged me to a first class
seat aboard despondency. Every semblance of hope and courage began to fade

into the backdrop of shame. My husband is wearing a translucent mask of guilt himself. He is the defender and protector of his brood. How could he fail Amos in such a tragic way? I feel completely responsible for his inability to rescue Amos. The burden of his guilt envelops me.

Another accomplice to guilt is "could have." The Saturday before the fire, I *could have* let another mother assume responsibility for the brunch and held my son all day long. I surely would have if I had known it was Amos's last day on earth.

What could have happened is only good for fiction. *What is* has all the real power. Guilt is a feeling of responsibility for wrongdoing. Even when we make mistakes, guilt should serve only one purpose: to make us correct our mistakes. After that, it has done its work. When guilt leads you to depression, it is stepping out of the intended boundary. The power of guilt overtakes us when we refuse to own up to our mistake or we have no desire to fix it.

> *Guilt is a powerful word. Even though it is not always a bad thing,*
> *it can make you or break you. It's best to try not to have guilt in your life.*
> —**Maria Martinez**, Amos House of Faith volunteer and burn survivor

In the case of irreversible, traumatic circumstances, when you are trying to move forward and pull out of the muck of guilt, "what ifs" can enable us to learn from our mistakes and not wallow in things beyond our control. But it's more productive to exchange "what ifs" and "could haves" with "what happened was" and "now I will." A careful distinction must be made between what was in your control and what was not.

The fire happened. I did not start the fire, and it is not my fault. The smoke detector did not have batteries; I will make sure that mistake is never repeated. I have come to terms with what I could have done and what I should have done.

One of Anne's lines in *Anne of Green Gables* resonates with me. Marilla confronts her about the whereabouts of her favorite brooch. Anne had put it on without asking but replaces it safely back on the pin cushion. As she gives her account of what happened, she admits her guilt in having the brooch without Marilla's consent. Then Anne says something I relate to: "The good thing about me is that I never make the same mistake twice."

I feel that way about the fire. I have vowed to keep fire safety precautions in the forefront. Guilt can be productive when we learn from our mistakes. When we unwillingly review the situation in our minds, what we did, and what happened as a result, an enormous feeling of regret can overshadow us. What we do with that emotion is the key to finding freedom from guilt.

You always have these thoughts in back of your mind: what if, I should have, I could have. Yet you realize it's too late. That guilt eats at you daily because you can't do anything about it. If only you could go back and change things—but you can't.

—**Tondra Edwards**, After Burns Club mom

Those in the burn-trauma circle may each be dealing with some level of guilt. The people who didn't get burned tend to experience survivor's guilt. That occurs when someone in the same tragic situation escapes death or injury that others suffered. They feel guilty that their life was spared, possibly at the expense of someone who was injured or didn't make it. They burden themselves with questions like, "Why was I the one who didn't get burned?" and "How come I wasn't able to get her out?"

A Note to Burn Survivors

One effective way to deal with survivor's guilt is to talk about it. Reality and guilt are tangled in your mind. Your unreasonable thoughts must be challenged. Talking with someone will put you in a position to straighten out the facts and avoid withdrawal; it may keep you from punishing yourself. It is also helpful to become supportive of the person you feel you have hurt.

Daniel, our autistic son, has a fork obsession. He hoards forks in his room and in the most unusual hiding places. When he first began this habit, we were constantly taking forks away from him: "No, Daniel, we use the forks to eat." One day, there was not one piece of silverware in the house. No forks, spoons, knives, or serving utensils. They had vanished. We were dumbfounded.

A little later that day, we heard Daniel's familiar clanking. Of course, he had two metal forks. Where he got them from was a mystery. We took them away, only to hear him, within thirty minutes, clanking two more forks together. I decided to play detective. Come to find out, Daniel had buried the silverware in an obscure place on the side of the house. Autistic children have brilliant minds. With suppressed grins, we reprimanded Daniel about the buried silverware, and life went on.

About a month later, I went in my silverware drawer and noticed that all of my soup spoons were gone.

"Daniel!" I yelled. "Show Mother where the soup spoons are!"

He came to me and just looked. I knew he had hidden them somewhere. We walked the perimeter of the yard. I was looking for a mound of dug up dirt.

We searched the entire house as Daniel clapped and hummed to himself, completely ignoring me. I was getting annoyed. I finally set him down and went into a long discourse about how he shouldn't take the spoons and how we need them to eat our cereal when Caleb wandered in the room.

He spoke in his usual direct manner, "Mother, I have the spoons. I put them in the car so we can get ice cream on the way back home tonight."

I felt so guilty. How do you apologize to an autistic child? How do you know he has forgiven you? I had judged him unfairly. Daniel was guilty by association.

Daniel and his fork fetish

A lot of burn survivors have been judged that way also—as if the reason they are on the unit is a result of a past deed. We can learn a lot from our children, can't we? I've learned that when guilt is unjustly laid at my door, I can respond as Daniel did: ignore it.

The burden of guilt you have for the mistakes you've made is heavy enough. No need to overload the wagon with unfounded accusations from others. People have a subtle way of imposing their perception of what happened on you, usually when they won't take responsibility for their own mistakes and the guilt that follows. Don't allow anyone to transfer their guilt to you.

My deepest feelings of guilt were resolved when I was able to be forgiven for what I had done and when I forgave myself. Both were equally important. Asking for forgiveness doesn't make you less of a person. It simply confirms the obvious: you are human. Forgiving yourself is usually the hardest. We don't like to think of ourselves as people with imperfections, but we are. Nevertheless, our fallacies don't have to keep us from being decent people. Guilt is in a tug of war with your future. Let it go, and fall to the ground so that you can move on.

Sis. Jones helps me into the new home she gave me

Prayer

Heavenly Father, I come to you in the name of Jesus. I feel horrible.
How could I not have put the batteries in the smoke detector?
I feel responsible for this whole nightmare. Now my son is gone.
Our lives will never be the same. I feel guilty about so many things.
I even feel bad about things that seemed out of my control.
I should have done something.
Forgive me for my mistakes.
Help others to forgive me as well.
In Jesus' name I pray,
Amen.

Chapter 12

THE GRIEVING PROCESS

Begin by admitting the truth—the pain,
anger, and helplessness you feel.

Allow the grieving process to take a natural course.

People are not likely to grieve the same way. That couldn't have been truer for me and my husband. I wanted pictures of Amos everywhere. It bothered him to see them. After the fire, when I was asked how many children I had, I would say six; he would say five. I didn't want Amos forgotten. He wanted to deal with the now. Whatever our own needs may be, there are several necessary components to the grieving process. They may occur in any order, but they are all necessary for healing and recovery.

It is common to revisit different stages multiple times during the process, and some stages may occur simultaneously. One thing that is helpful for you to do for

107

yourself is to begin by admitting the truth—the pain, anger, and helplessness you feel. Allow the grieving process to take a natural course.

When I was a little girl, our family had a dog named Wolfie. Wolfie was half German shepherd and half wolf. He was a strange dog to me, with peculiar ways. This dog would actually howl at the moon every night for hours. I thought he was a nuisance. My younger sister Stacy loved him to death.

Wolfie loved to chase people for fun. Of course, if you were the stranger being chased, it wasn't amusing. My mother would always warn Stacy about not tying him up. Stacy was a little mischievous. I think she got a kick out of seeing people being chased. Wolfie really was pretty nice to people once he got to know them.

Her biggest problem was with how people treated Stacy. She loved Stacy as much as Stacy loved her—probably even more. Wolfie was fiercely protective over her. Stacy and the mail carrier didn't exactly see eye to eye. Stacy always wanted to get the mail, and the mailman thought she was too little to get it. Wolfie could sense the tension between them.

One day the mailman raised his voice, not very loud, but loud enough to draw Wolfie's attention. She broke from her leash, chased the mailman, and bit him. I can still hear Stacy's cries: "No Wolfie, bad Wolfie! Why did you do that?"

Wolfie contracted rabies and had to be euthanized. Stacy cried and sulked for weeks. I could not understand that reaction for the life of me. In my eyes, she was just a dog and a bad one at that. What I saw was relief from the work it took to feed her, bathe her, and take her walking. Stacy's perspective was totally different. She had lost a close friend, her dog, a companion that was company and that reciprocated her love. She was grieving. Although I didn't say much, I wasn't any help to her either because I didn't understand.

This is the place that a lot of people are at when they cannot relate to what you've been through; they are void of understanding. I understood the simple surface problem. Stacy's dog died. Just like people understood the surface problem with us. She got burned. But the depths of the impact will go over others' heads until they become intimately connected to your heart issues.

I've learned not to be offended by a person's ignorance, realizing that there are many things about which I am ignorant as well. Ignorance has an unfair connotation associated with it. Many people are offended by the use of the word. It is often misinterpreted to mean foolish. There is a great difference between the two. Ignorance just means you lack education or knowledge about something. Foolish is when you will not apply what you know. My tolerance for foolishness is not as high. I was ignorant concerning the depths of Stacy's feeling, but I wasn't foolish. I knew the basics; she was badly hurt and needed consolation. An encouragement to caregivers and visitors: that's all you need to know as well when your loved one is grieving.

Most people are not prepared for the grief that follows a sudden tragedy that strikes like a thief in the night. You swing from one extreme to another. The first dose of emotional narcotics we give ourselves to ease the pain is denial. Denial gives you the leisure not to deal with anything. It is one of the stages most often revisited during the grieving process.

During my personal grieving process, I fellowshipped with denial quite frequently. I remember telling myself in the hospital, within the first few hours that I woke up, that everybody had to have made it. Despite the chaos and severity of the situation, it hurt too much to consider that someone had actually died. Even though the count for the boys never passed five, I told myself they had to have gotten Amos out. Denial allowed me a few more moments to enjoy Amos's life. It kept the tip of the dagger that had pierced my hurt from plunging all the way through. To admit his death to myself was equivalent to emotional suicide.

Denial reminds me of playing pretend as children. I really liked to pretend because you didn't even need another person with you to play it. I could come up with the most elaborate situations. I have been creative for as long as I can remember. I remember a common thread in all of my imaginary situations. There was always a loving father. He was a handsome father who was present and loved me. My game was kind of sad when you think about it. It was another form of denial. The sadder thing was that when the game was over, the father disappeared. At that point, reality set in. The more I pretended, the greater the reality affected me. Not until I stopped pretending was I able to adjust safely to what truly was.

> *Grief is something you cannot begin to describe. Unfortunately, you have to experience it to understand. It really hurts—not just your broken heart, but deep down in your bones, in your stomach, everywhere. There is no way to prepare, no goodbyes, and it hurts. What are we supposed to do with the emptiness that follows? You and I have chosen to be proactive about fire safety, which has helped me heal since Ben's death. I know I am a survivor, so I know that God will show me what I can do to heal again.*
>
> —**Bonnie Woodruff**, Common Voices advocate; lost son Ben Woodruff in University of North Carolina fraternity fire

Anger is the stage that was most difficult for me. Anger caused me to be withdrawn, to coil up like a snake, and then lash out at those who were there to help me. During this stage, I remember transferring the guilt that I felt to other people, some of whom had nothing to do with our fire. Nurses, doctors, therapists, and family members had to step lightly around me. Sometimes they could do nothing right. As unfair as it is, the salve needed during this period is patience and understanding.

Anger was not a foreign emotion to me. I have always had to concentrate on controlling it. It was magnified during the fire. It is not uncommon for a patient on the unit to be angry and have no clear idea of why. The base reasons are simple: You are displeased. You don't like what is going on. You are hurt or offended by the present situation. So, what's wrong with anger anyway? Nothing if we use it to get positive things accomplished. Everything changes, however, when it moves us to afflict ourselves and others.

Even though it is emotionally painful, grief is a healing process. That is why it is so important to allow people space to grieve. No one wants to see his or her loved one suffer or in pain. The reality is this causes pain for you. Many caregivers have a tendency to attempt to rush the process for their loved ones, in order to keep their own suffering at a minimum.

This is unhealthy because it pushes the patient to act on a level they have not reached.

I remember being visited in the hospital by a dear friend who was used to our time together being full of laughter. This particular day when she came by, I was trapped in the bargaining stage. I had been thinking about Amos and how I wished he could have lived instead of me. I was running one scenario after another. There were times, especially when the twins wanted to sleep with us, that they would sit up in their beds, looking at us with those adorable, brown eyes, holding their Thomas the Train blankets. Why wasn't March seventh one of those times? If the twins had been sleeping with us, then my husband could have thrown them out first.

The first thing I blurted out when she came in the room was, "I wish I was dead and not Amos."

It wasn't the normal witty joke or humor she was accustomed to. For a quick second, she was in shock and didn't know what to say. After she recovered, she sat on the edge of my bed and held both of my hands in hers.

In her attempt to help me, she made a damaging remark: "You can't break down. If you break down, everyone else will too."

I didn't want to be responsible for everyone else's sadness. So I dried my tears and told her thank you. What I wanted to say, however, was, "Are you nuts?"

Of course, at night I was alone and free to feel whatever I felt. So I would get back on my scenario train and ride until the next morning. Feelings are neither right nor wrong; they just are. We have to be accountable for the actions we take, no matter how we are feeling.

After you have crossed over denial, plowed through anger, and lost at bargaining, you find yourself landing in the field of depression. It may seem that you are starting all over again. Nevertheless, this can be an incredibly beneficial stage to travel through. This stage indicates that you are considering the harsh realities of your situation for what they are. Even though you don't like it, you are ripe for acceptance.

This stage can last the longest. It is not easy to process or accept losing everything you ever owned. It is difficult to accept death, disfigurement, emotional scaring, or financial pain as the result of one event—especially when you are broadsided. The drug of choice for me during this stage was sleep. It allowed me an emotional escape from it all. Many people lose their appetite at this point.

Who can put a time cap on your grieving process? No one. You may grieve one day, or you may never stop grieving. What's most important is that you get to the final stage: acceptance. It is so crucial because when you rise from this stage, you have accepted the tragedy as fact and are ready to move forward.

The one thing our family didn't do, which I feel was a grave mistake, was grieve our loss together. We are all such private, strong, independent people— even the kids. I, of course, grieved with my husband alone or with one of the kids one-on-one (as he also did). The boys even shared times together. But as a whole family unit, we never sat in one place, at one time, and just cried together. It's really strange, particularly because we have spent so much of our lives all together openly sharing. I feel a time like that could have circumvented a lot of repressed feelings, validated others, and helped all of us to heal inwardly.

Page Family 2003

Most importantly, it is a blessing when your feelings are validated at every stage and when you have support. Judging is so damaging. I have actually overheard caregivers say insane things about their loved ones like, "You would think she would be over this by now; it was just a burn," or "I know it can't hurt that bad." Talk about inciting a burn survivor's anger!

A Note to Caregivers

A bit of advice to caregivers and visitors: don't speak lightly on matters you don't understand. Keep compassion and mercy in the forefront, no matter how things appear—especially in the case of death. Flippant comments like, "At least you have five other boys," as if Amos didn't matter, were hurtful.

The loss of my son had me scrambling for peace and understanding. During the initial stages of my grieving process, I wanted to talk about him. It was therapeutic for me to remember him, what he did, and what he liked. He was gone, but my love for him was very much alive.

> *Thou shalt not be a victim; thou shalt not be a perpetrator.*
> *But above all, thou shalt not be a bystander.*
> —**Gail Minger**, Common Voices advocate; lost son Michael Minger
> in an arson dormitory fire at Murray State University in Kentucky

Suppressing your grief only makes it worse when it finally comes out. Suppressed grief is like rice boiling in a pot too long with the lid on. Eventually, it will boil over, raising the lid and causing water and rice to fall all over the place. Grief can get so heavy at times that you feel you will die from the heaviness.

I have come to understand that grief will even out to a bearable level with time. What we need during the most intense time is consolation. It may come from a family member, a friend, or a stranger. Accept it when it is offered. My church family and husband were great consolers, but Jesus was my ultimate consolation, the God of all consolation (2 Cor. 1:3).

Prayer

Heavenly Father, I come to you in the name of Jesus.

The grief is so heavy. I am not sure I can handle it.

Why do things have to be this way?

I want Amos back, but I know that is not possible.

Help me. I feel myself spiraling downward,

but I know you are the lifter of my head.

It seems like no one understands, but I know you do.

You are touched by the feelings of our infirmities.

I will take my consolation in you.

You are the God of all consolation.

In Jesus' name,

Amen.

Chapter 13

FORGIVENESS

It may not be my fault, but it is surely
my problem when I choose not to forgive.

By January of 1991, our family had not reached the impressive size it was destined to become. In anticipation of increasing our offspring, my husband, two sons, and I were looking to transfer from our snug, two-bedroom apartment to a home with a fence and yard. We needed a space where the boys could romp and run, so buying a home was our intention. It seemed as if we had looked at a million homes from the time Joseph was born until February of that year.

One day when I was out on the hunt, I ran across a sign in a yard that said "House for Rent." It was a four-bedroom, two-bath house with a formal living and dining room, kitchen, den, and garage. The yard was fenced and gigantic.

*James Page Jr. & sons
Jonathon & Joseph*

It seemed like a spacious place for four people. As I sat in front of the house, I began to envision a space I could use for a classroom. I quickly jotted down the number and raced home to share the news with my husband.

It was a done deal. Our new home would be 4151 Sue Ellen. There was no lease. My husband and Mr. Guillory sealed the contract on a handshake—a verbal commitment, their word of honor being the foundation each stood on. We moved into the home on my husband's birthday, March 4, 1991. Our game plan was to stay there for a year or two—enough time to save up for the dream home we desired.

Before we knew it, four more sons were added to the crew, and we had spent eight years on Sue Ellen. Mr. Guillory made it especially appealing to stay. He was quick to do any repairs that were needed. He also had a generous way about him. He would show up at the house with a turkey at Thanksgiving or a ham at Christmas or just chocolate for mom. He even started a savings account for our three oldest boys. It was obvious that he was smitten with the kids.

We did not see him as the landlord but as a favored family friend. The fire threatened to shred that friendship to pieces. Even though the source of the fire was never officially declared, the cause of the fire still existed. Behind that cause was a person to blame—someone to hold accountable. The death of a child, injury of multiple family members, and the total destruction of a home is a massive burden to put on any human's shoulder. Mr. Guillory took that load upon himself.

Periodically, my husband would pass on messages from Mr. Guillory and his inquiries about how Ben and I were doing. I acknowledged them verbally, but inwardly I ignored them. I knew he was seeking forgiveness. I wasn't ready to release him. I secretly blamed Mr. Guillory, even though I never voiced it. I couldn't say anything; the man had done everything he could for us. Yet I couldn't help but remember the gray tape that covered some wires in the attic my husband told me about. He had asked Mr. Guillory to take a look at it. It was the one thing he never did. I concluded that the cause of the fire was the faulty wiring in the attic, the wires that Mr. Guillory neglected to look into. It was all his fault.

Forgiveness is a huge deal. It is one of the most difficult challenges we face as humans. Nobody wants to do it, yet everyone desires it. The act of dispensing forgiveness may seem impossible. But, its delivery results in freedom. Unforgiveness destroys the vessel that contains it. It robs you of peace. It is like a rude bill collector. It will mentally harass you, demanding payment from those who cannot afford to pay. What could Mr. Guillory possibly do to right our tragedy? Nothing.

Eventually, I decided simply to forgive him. Unforgiveness wasn't producing anything worth waiting on. It took real work to abide in unforgiveness. You have to remember the offense. Then you have to come up with a penalty. Then you have to make sure it is carried out. This process was way too much work for me, especially with all the other things I was dealing with.

For the person of faith, forgiveness is a requirement. There is no way around it. Forgive that you may be forgiven (). That command doesn't necessarily make the process more appealing, but there is an awesome advantage. We can draw strength and resolve from the reality that Christ forgave us. What a liberating experience that is! We also have God's Spirit to assist us. It empowers us to "do unto others as you would have them do unto you" (). However, when we are trespassed against, especially in a horrific manner, it is hard to keep the Golden Rule front of mind.

This is especially true when we cannot imagine ourselves committing the very ghastly acts that have been done to us. In these instances, we do not relate to the perpetrator at all. Forgiving the person seems like a joke. When I think about my accusation against Mr. Guillory, the charges can be summarized as the following: he forgot to check or he never took time to check the wire in the attic. It was a simple mistake with a devastating cost.

As I thought further, I realized my family could lay a similar charge at my door. I forgot to check or I never took time to check the batteries in the smoke detector, which contributed to the same result. It was another simple mistake with a devastating cost. In that light, in acknowledging my own fault, it was easier to follow the Golden Rule. It was easier to forgive Mr. Guillory just as I desired my family to forgive me.

I was at home in the den, reclining on my comfortable, cream leather sectional, enjoying the sight of the boys playing with the remote control trucks and the puzzles that had been donated to them. The contours on the sectional were particularly comfortable, considering the burns on my back. The phone rang and Jonathon and Caleb raced to answer it.

"Page residence," Jonathon answered in his adult voice. "Hi, Daddy . . . Yes sir . . . Just a minute. Mother, it's Daddy Man."

It was not the conversation I expected. My husband had called to tell me that Mr. Guillory wanted to see me. He wanted to apologize face-to-face. I had made a conscientious decision to forgive him, but the idea of seeing him made me question the sincerity of my proclamation.

It was six thirty that evening, and Mr. Guillory was expected to arrive at seven o'clock. My husband had made it home from work, dinner was finished, and the boys were in their rooms playing. My stomach was in knots. I had no idea what I would say or do. I was nervous because I knew myself. When I am confronted, I will tell the truth, with no details spared. I express exactly what I feel. How did I really feel about this man?

At seven sharp, there was a knock at the door. I smiled in spite of myself. Mr. Guillory, always punctual and a man of his word—except the one time I needed him most. The emotional tug of war began before he even got inside of the door. My husband embraced him in the foyer for a long period of time. I overheard him telling Mr. Guillory that it was all right; we are okay. My heart softened. It was a tough road and a long journey ahead of us, but we were coming out as victors. We were okay. God was taking care of us in a miraculous way.

In an instant of clarity, I realized that Mr. Guillory was not okay. He was wounded, deeply sorry, and desperate for forgiveness. He entered the den where I was sitting and froze. His eyes were red and watery, and he didn't utter a word. His trepidation was apparent. My heart went out to him. I held the key to the prison door he had enclosed himself in. I had the words he desperately needed to hear.

Without thinking twice, I waved him over, and we embraced. It didn't even have to be said. We were basking in a sea of forgiveness. The currents were electrifying. It was a simple decision that eased the tension of a complex situation; it was the decision to forgive.

Then Ben wandered into the room. His trachea was in at that time, and he had on his black pressure garments: a full face mask, gloves, and arm wear. He looked like a miniature ninja. True to his character, he stood front and center of Mr. Guillory, waving, demanding a response. Mr. Guillory picked him up and held him and the tears flowed. By the end of the visit, everyone was refreshed. Forgiveness had washed all of our souls.

Some people are forgiving by nature. I was not. Forgiveness was actually contrary to the nature I was born with and lived out growing up. My ability to forgive was not of myself. It was the transformation that Christ did in my life that enabled me to forgive.

During my school age days and especially my high school years, I was notorious for holding a grudge. Consequently, I spent a great many of my high school days miserable on the inside, waiting for an opportune moment to get my vengeance. It was an unfortunate and burdensome way to live. Justice is what I called it. Foolishness is what it was. It didn't help that I had a memory like an elephant. I would not forget, and I would not forgive. You had to pay, and I had to execute the judgment. It was the only way I felt vindicated.

With all the activities I was involved in and as busy as my life was, you would think that I didn't even have time to carry a grudge, much less plan vengeful acts. Unfortunately, all I needed was a moment. My mind was a continual rolling wheel. I was always thinking. Even in my sleep, I dreamed often. My unforgiving attitude transferred itself to solid grudges. I harbored that resentment until the point of vengeance. The vengeance I administered tainted my character. That is one of the most potent dangers of unforgiveness: its ability to mar your character. When mingled together in a person's heart, the mixture of grudges and vengeance can change the good nature you have into something shameful.

It was my best friend's birthday. We were in junior high school. We were attending the summer youth sports program during a scorching summer in Kansas City, Missouri. My buddy was upset and irritated. She felt no one remembered her birthday but me. I was privy to the fact that her parents were planning an elaborate surprise birthday party for her that evening. I didn't let on I knew anything.

By the time we got on the bus to head home, she was irate. She made a simple statement that caused me to remember a long-standing grudge: "I could just hit somebody." Instantly, a memory came to mind. It was the first day of the program. I was standing in line, waiting on my turn to get a drink from the water fountain. When I bowed my head to take a sip, another girl in my group pushed me away. I stepped back to the fountain and finished getting my drink as she mocked me and had the whole group laughing at me.

Before I wiped the water from my mouth, I had vowed in my heart to get her back. The grudge was rooted in mere seconds. She was sitting on the same bus with us. My heart experienced a twisted peace. I pointed her out to my friend and said, "Let's get her." The end of the story is too shameful to rehearse. Unforgiveness that sits in the heart and is allowed to fester can produce actions that are just as reprehensible as the action that was done to you.

Unforgiveness makes you a prisoner of the past. Don't allow anything in the past to rob you of your future. Don't miss the blessing of what is before you by marinating in the past. The pain of what happened is enough. When you dwell in unforgiveness, you give the perpetrator power to abuse you over and over again.

When I was in second grade, we moved from Los Angeles to Kansas City. My hair had been over-processed and was short and uneven. My grandmother was out of solutions for what to do for my hair that day, so she unwisely put my great grandmother's gray and black peppered wig on me. Off to school I went, looking totally ridiculous. The laughter and taunting from the kids was instantaneous.

The cruelest ridicule took place on the playground. While I was standing near the jungle gym, waiting for my turn to get on, Cedric, Alexander, and Sammy Lewis (yes, I still remember them by name) stood a little distance behind me and took a long stick and threw my wig up in a nearby tree. I was beyond humiliation and embarrassment. I can still to this day see the children sprawled about on the asphalt, holding their stomachs laughing at me.

Unforgiveness had settled in my little heart so strongly that I was a senior in high school before I stopped inflicting pain and vengeance on them. It took me a while to understand that no matter how I hurt them, the episode was not erased. My senior year, I made a decision to just drop it. I was the one continually bringing it to the forefront. They were sorry for the incident many years back. It wasn't till I was a few months shy of my high school graduation that I was able to tell that story and laugh myself.

Here is a hard reality: humans have a way of really hurting and offending each other. Sometimes it's intentional, but many times it is not. Whatever the case, we instinctively know how to deliver blows where the impact is most destructive. The closer you are in a relationship, the deeper the pain can travel. A stranger's misdoing can only go so far. But when the offense comes from a family member, spouse, church member, or best friend, the blow can floor you.

Some women are on the burn unit facing multiple amputations because their husbands set them on fire or threw acid on them. These men were purposely trying to disfigure their wives out of pure spite and jealousy. Some children are on the burn unit with facial disfigurement because their parents scalded them as infants in an attempt to end their precious lives.

Teenagers have banded together against one child, pouring gas on him with no other intention than to inflict pain on someone they wanted to control. Most children do not realize the full implications of their actions. The number of atrocities is staggering.

Does forgiveness have a place in these situations? Yes, even though it is a formidable task. It may not appear so, but the person forgiving benefits the most from the action of forgiving. When you forgive, your work is over. You have figuratively dumped the whole messy situation in the other person's lap and given him the responsibility to handle it.

Often the trespasser mistakes forgiveness for a declaration that what was done was not wrong or that it was okay in the eyes of the person trespassed against. That couldn't be further from the truth. That is not what forgiveness is at all. Forgiveness says what you did was despicable, but I will not be the one trying to collect payment. It is now between you and God; he is requiring payment for this case. In many ways, forgiveness performs the duties of a prosecuting attorney. It gets the facts, does the research, presents the case, speaks, and wins for you.

> *Forgiveness is not a "process" but is instantly granted by an act of one's will. Dealing with the emotions that continuously resurface from the memory of the offense and the pain it causes is a process.*
> **—Deirdra Curry**, friend

I try to look at forgiveness this way. I have already survived the offense. Why sit there and hold it? In an effort to move forward and to keep going, I let it go. Unforgiveness is too heavy. It slows you down.

As a former track competitor, I know how important it is to dress in lightweight clothes and not be weighted down if you want to win the gold. If you want to win the race called life, forgiveness is a legal steroid that will give you the advantage. It all starts in the mind. What we think is what we will do. Thoughts release themselves into the heart and produce actions that shape our character.

True forgiveness takes a well-made-up mind. It takes a determination to release the other person from the penalty and payment of the debt owed. I knew true forgiveness had taken place the next time we went to visit Mr. Guillory at his daughter's house. For one, I did not have any hesitation to go. There was no uneasiness or anger. We had returned to a familiar place. But just because forgiveness takes place, it doesn't mean that the memories that came with the offense are erased.

Forgiveness is not a hocus-pocus game where everything is all right because we waved a magic wand. We will always be conscious of what happened and who did what. The power of forgiveness is what we do with that knowledge. When we decide to chain someone to his past mistake, we must remember the other cuff is on us. It may not be my fault, but it is surely my problem when I choose not to forgive.

Prayer

Heavenly Father, I come to you in the name of Jesus.
Our Father, which art in heaven. Hallowed be thy name.
Thy kingdom come. Thy will be done on earth
as it is in heaven. Give us this day our daily bread
and forgive us our debt as we forgive our debtors (Matt. 6:9-12).
Lord, help. I know I need to forgive. It is so difficult to do so right now.
It doesn't even seem fair. Please help me to remember
that I have hurt others before and have needed their forgiveness.
Most of all, I need your forgiveness.
I will forgive through the strength you supply.
I can do all things through Christ who strengthens me.
Lead me not into temptation, but deliver me from all evil.
For thine is the kingdom and the glory forever (6:13).
In Jesus' name,
Amen.

Chapter 14

RELATIONSHIP DYNAMICS

There is a friend that sticketh closer than a brother.
Proverbs 18:24

My church family was there at the onset of the tragedy. Many were at the scene on Sue Ellen, some at the hospital before the ambulances arrived, and the others came shortly after. They began an immediate prayer covering for us.

Within a few hours, the hospital was filled with family members and friends who had flown in from our hometown in Missouri. They completely took over the waiting area. The response to our tragedy was so great that the staff thought I was a local hometown celebrity. I was not. I was an unknown in Houston who happened to be in a local church body founded on love.

Benjamin and I went from the ambulance straight to surgery. My husband was told the doctors were trying to save our lives. I can't begin to imagine how he felt. His parents and blood relatives were more than nine hundred miles away in St. Louis. My family was an equal distance away in Kansas City. They were booking flights and jumping in vans to get to Houston as quickly as they could, but he would have had at least three hours alone, waiting on family.

Our out-of-state loved ones were not able to stay for our entire hospitalization and understandably so, as we were in the hospital for months. They continued to show their support through prayer, calls, and financial assistance.

The blessing James had in that tragic hour was the church family of Full Gospel Church of Love In Christ. The congregation was right there beside him, praying, loving, caring, and seeing him through. Everyone assumed a role, bearing an extra responsibility just to make sure we were taken care of. Their spontaneity to assume this role was as natural as the sunrise. We had an intimate relationship.

Close relationships are not confined to blood relatives. There is a friend who will stick closer than a brother. In the dark hours of your tragedy, when you need so much help, family are the people who respond. My drive and determination to help others is a direct result of the thankfulness I have for the love and support my church family gave.

Families gave up their vacations in order to help us. While I was in the hospital, I never lacked visitors, food, snacks, or anything they thought I wanted. My children were well taken care of, day and night. My husband was free to visit us as he willed. It was an honor to have the local church body display so great a light of love in this manner.

> *If I had to do it all again, I would in a heartbeat. It was instantaneous love when I saw you in the hospital bed the first time. I told you then and there you wouldn't see me every day because I would take care of the family. I did just that and would do it AGAIN.*
> **—Sheila Cotton**, friend

Many years ago, my sister-in-law in Memphis had an accident that injured her leg so badly she wasn't able to work. I called and asked her about moving in with us for a while until she got back on her feet. She was a bit reluctant because she didn't want to be a burden to her brother's new family. She is an independent lady and was used to taking care of herself.

I finally persuaded her to come to Texas so we could take care of her, ensuring her that she would not be a burden. From the day she stepped foot into our home till the day she left, she did nothing but take care of us and "her babies" as she called them. Every family should be blessed with an Aunt Jackie. We never had to ask her to do anything. She did what she saw needed to be done. Before I got out of bed, breakfast was made and the kids were bathed and fed. The kids loved her.

I had it so easy when she lived with us that I was actually ashamed of myself. I had to ask her not to do so much. We never had to give her much either. She would find some kind of work and contribute. If we didn't take it, she would give it to the kids. We had an amazing relationship dynamic working as sisters-in-law. At the core of it was a mutual respect and genuine gratefulness. I was grateful for her thoughtfulness and kindness. The way she would send us away on date nights or just take the boys on outings so I could get some rest was greatly appreciated.

She respected my position in the household as wife and mother of the kids. I respected her individuality. I never assumed she had to do anything for me and mine. As I pondered the success we had as two grown women living in the same house, I gained a lot of wisdom from my relationship with Aunt Jackie. The basic principles we had working between us are working dynamics that would make any relationship successful. Trust, honesty, and communication are amongst our top relationship markers.

One of the courses I took in my electrical engineering program was dynamics. Dynamics is the study of the motion of bodies, anything with mass. Relationship dynamics is about movement, progression, and change. When a family member is severely injured, change may be necessary to keep things moving and relationships progressing. The male in the family, who was the primary bread winner, may have been injured. The wife may be forced to assume that role for a period of time so that the family is sustained.

This is a difficult spot that many male burn survivors find themselves in. Many men pride themselves in providing for their families. A good way to boost his morale in this uncomfortable situation is by emphasizing all the other contributions he is making in the household. Another bit of advice is to let him assume as much responsibility as he can. Even if it is tasks you normally like to do. No one wants to feel useless.

Be mindful that when a burn trauma happens to a family member, every person in the family is affected. We are visual people by nature. There is a tendency for us to focus on the family members with the visible scars.

This was especially true with our family. Benjamin and I received a great deal of attention. However, emotional trauma and scars need just as much attention. Ignoring the needs of the other siblings or spouse can create animosity and grow contempt.

No relationship is perfect. Don't automatically assume that the difficulties you are experiencing in your relationships are centered around your scars or disfigurement. Many of our difficulties began long ago.

I had an embarrassing problem for years. I did not care to develop close bonds with short males. And God forbid if one asked me out on a date. It was a major offense. What in the world was wrong with me? Why in the world did I have difficulty having relationships as simple as friendship with a short man?

I have been right at six feet since I was in fifth grade. My thinness at that time made me look seven feet tall. I was teased mercilessly about my height during my elementary and junior high years. Just standing by a short male made me feel taller. It accentuated my flaw, my height. I am no longer self-conscious about my height; therefore, I don't have any more issues being with short men. When you experience a burn trauma, you don't leave your issues at the site of the fire, you bring them with you to the hospital room.

Relationships are sustained or deteriorate through the ways we relate to each other. The way we relate to one another is a direct reflection of our perception and internal thoughts toward one another. There is a line in a movie that speaks to this point perfectly. The relationship between the mother and son is strained. They are a wealthy family with a lucrative business. The son has struck a risky business deal that forces the mother to sell a portion of her shares in the company to keep the business above water. This puts her son in a powerful position and compromises her status and position on the board.

When she unwillingly agrees to do so, at the counsel of her trusted COO, a big grin spreads across the son's face. She shoots him a pointed look. He responds by saying, "What, Mother, you don't trust me?" She responds with a revealing statement about most of mankind: "It is your private thoughts that give me pause."

Many of us relate to our family, friends, and enemies in this same manner. We are responsive to what we perceive as the person's true intentions. It doesn't matter much about what he or she is actually saying. Many times what a person is not saying is the statement that speaks the loudest.

> *There are so many relationships that one develops throughout his or her lifetime. Each relationship has a life of its own, and each changes as time goes on. Relationships will have high points and low points; it is within each of those times and what is done during those times that help make the relationship what it is. Communication is key in having a healthy relationship with anyone (mother, father, spouse, friend).*
> —**Christine Jurus**, burn survivor, Phoenix Society for Burn Survivors

I think the spousal relationship is the hardest relationship to keep intact during a tragedy. The relationship James and I had survived this tragedy by the grace of God. What could have torn us apart bonded us together more strongly. We were close before the fire. We drew closer after the fire. Before the fire, I felt he really loved me. At the end of the tragedy, I knew he really loved me. My respect for him was heightened by the commitment he had for me and the boys.

The incident brought our marriage to a different level of maturity. I was blessed to have him by my side. I can still see where things could have not turned out so well. I see different areas we could have dipped into that would have torn us apart. Blaming each other for what happened is a major one.

Many spousal relationships rip at the seams behind the blame game: "This would never have happened if," or "Amos is gone because you." Then anger would have crept in, and animosity would have taken us both down. Lack of patience is another big risk factor. My husband needed to be patient with me.

There was a lot to deal with. I had physical issues, emotional issues, and all kind of needs. The kids needed help. The man was swamped.

I had to exercise patience as well. With so many things to take care of, I had to wait patiently for things to get done. Giving up is the major risk. I have seen spouses just walk away, as if they never knew the person. It is a tragic thing to behold when someone has no endurance and is unable to hold on. My husband and I wanted a future together. It didn't matter if that future would include scars, death, and disfigurement. We wanted to stay together.

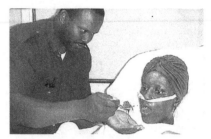

James feeding his wife on Burn Unit

Never let anyone or anything determine who you are or what your life should be. You are the one to set the bar on your future
—**Cheryl Williams**, burn survivor, LVN at Seton Heart Institute

Losing a brother affected the way the boys related to each other in a powerful way. The most interesting thing that I noticed was that they did not argue. They always got along. They never screamed or raised their voices against one another. Even my friends noticed. The fact that you can be here today and gone tomorrow was not a cliché but a reality in their minds. They felt that anybody could die at any time. It matured them greatly. They were glad to have each other.

A common pitfall for sibling relationships is jealousy, especially if either of the parents is showing more attention to a particular child. Jealousy will change the way you look at a person. When you look at a person with a jealous eye, everything he does is wrong. It is important to take care of the needs of all the children, injured or not. That will keep jealousy from overtaking them.

Thank God we have each other.
—**Jonathon Page**

Relationships can't be forced—no matter how noble the intent is. If a person doesn't want to be bothered, he won't be. You cannot make people like you. Neither should you try. I've watched people try to buy relationships, only to be bitterly disappointed in the end. It takes two people to build any type relationship. Time has to be put in to make it last. Each person has to bring something to the table.

Amos House of Faith 2009
Fire Safety Obstacle Course

Fire Safety Obstacle Course Winner

Smokey (A-K-A Caleb Page) at
Fire Safety Obstacle Course

Smokey gives mom a hug

Prayer

Jesus, please safeguard all of my relationships.
Bless my husband with peace and strength.
Help the boys to get along.
Help my friends to understand where I am.
Help me to understand them as well.
I feel like I have nothing to offer to anyone.
Give me something to bring to the table.
Help me to be honest in all my relations.
In Jesus' name,
Amen.

Chapter 15

ACCEPTANCE ISSUES

When I accept me it is easier for others to do the same.

I vividly remember sitting on the marble shower bench in our bathroom as my husband gingerly gave me my shower. We both seemed to be in our own worlds, he concentrating on the task at hand as my mind searched to figure out his thoughts. I was unable to use my hands at the time, so cleaning and dressing my wounds during my shower was one of the items on his long lists of responsibilities.

As I watched him lather the rag and hum to himself, I could not help but think that the sores, bruises, and burns were disgusting to him. I wanted to know his true feelings. It seemed he was consumed with protecting mine. Myriad questions kept flowing through my mind: *What does he think of me now? Is he able to look at me without feeling queasy? Would he ever want to hold me again? How ugly and gross am I?*

My thoughts were interrupted by the soft touch of my husband's hand on my chin. He used his thumb to wipe away the trickle of tears that had escaped without my notice. As if he had been given a direct line to my jumbling thoughts, he answered my questions with one statement.

He spoke with a sincerity that touched me deeply and simply said, "You are so beautiful." Then he leaned in and gave me a tender kiss on the scar on my face.

The torrent of tears that followed was a mixture of relief, hope, and utter gratefulness for this man. I felt the soothing satisfaction of acceptance. At that point, it didn't matter to me how anyone else felt.

One of a burn survivor's biggest hurdles to cross is the issue of acceptance. This is especially true as it relates to those he loves most. Parents, spouses, children, and best friends are in a powerful position to build or destroy your self-esteem during this assailable time.

Benjamin enjoys the pig race at the Houston Rodeo

At the burn center where I was treated, mirrors were not kept in the room. This is a common practice for most burn centers throughout the country. The pain and anxiety of living is in the forefront. What you look like or smell like is totally insignificant for some time. At some point, however, it eventually dawns on you that you have no idea how you look.

This is especially true for facial burns. I had first and second degree burns on my face. I found myself trying to gage how horrible I looked by the expressions on the faces of first-time visitors. First-time visitors were not guarded, and it usually took a few seconds for them to recover from the shock of what they saw.

Friends and loved ones prepare themselves emotionally for the visit, determined to be a strength and comfort. They wipe away the tears, plant a pleasant expression on their face, and enter the room. In the first few seconds, however, reality wins the tug of war, and they respond to what they see. A faltering smile, wide eyes, and hesitation to continue into the room are all nonverbal cues that persuade me that I look horrible.

I haven't seen my face yet, so my acceptance of my appearance rests on the precarious slope of my visitors' reactions. After the first few seconds, their actions are back in check. The smile returns, and you are asked in a concerned voice, "How are you feeling?"

I respond, "Fine. Thank you for coming by." Inwardly, I'm wounded and wondering about my present reality.

My self-esteem was obliterated by the time I reached kindergarten. I was the middle daughter of five siblings. My two brothers were oldest, and I was sandwiched between the three younger girls. My baby sister was adorable; my older sister was gorgeous; and then there was me. I was ugly. I had heard it from many sources and overhead it from others, so at the immature age of five, I accepted it as fact. I consoled myself in the fact that I was smart and funny. My peers agreed.

No one could tell me different. No one could tell me I was pretty or beautiful either. They could say the words audibly, but it would not go any further than the space of the breath that it took to say it. My heart could not receive it. I had built a wall of protection that was impossible to penetrate for many years. I was terrified of being hurt and rejected by slights about my appearance.

This was a major problem in high school. I would not date like your normal teenager. I didn't believe my suitors were serious. I have only had three dates in my entire life, and I only accepted them to appease my friends. The low self-esteem went further than anyone knew. I had a secret. I would not look in mirrors if it was at all possible. I did not like what I saw. I did not like me. I mastered combing my hair without mirrors. I'm probably the only female in the world that did that.

Sister Jones discovered my secret. How, I do not know. She was the one who coerced me into looking in the mirror and accepting myself for the beautiful person that God had made me. It's sad but that is why the scars on my body didn't have a profound effect on me. I had been accustomed to feeling ugly for a long time. I dropped back into that place easily. My husband's love and acceptance, however, was able to pull me out.

One of the most exhilarating times in my life was when my nurse and the child-life staff arranged a time and meeting space for me to see my four oldest children for the first time after the fire. I couldn't even sleep the night before.

I was strapped in my neuro chair—a chair to acclimate patients to sitting up after being on their backs for a long time—and for the first time, I was anxious to be in it. Sitting in the neuro chair was an excruciatingly painful experience. Sitting up was torturous to the nerves, and the norm at that phase in my recovery was to watch the clock so that I could hurry and get back in bed. The ventilator was gone, but there was still an assortment of tubes in my nose, in my arms, and generally hanging everywhere. That didn't matter. I was about to see the people who loved me most and loved me unconditionally.

My husband had come and dressed me in a purple satin house dress. Purple would put me in a good mood on any kind of day. My hair had been braided, and I was wild with anticipation. My husband wheeled me away from the confinement of my room, and every space gained felt like a sprint toward independence and freedom.

When we got to the entrance of the appointed room, my husband paused, kissed me on my cheek, and asked me if I was ready. I closed my eyes, savoring the moment, shook my head yes, and then the doors swung open. My autistic son ran from me so quickly that all I could see was a blurred image passing by. My husband had to sprint to catch him.

When I turned and looked at the three older boys, I was mortified. Caleb had an alarming, disgusted look on his face and was backing away from me. Joseph was frozen as if he were in a trance and afraid to move or do anything. My expectation of grand acceptance evaporated instantly. It was the worst rejection I had ever experienced in my life. It felt as if someone had poured cold water on my head. I was so hurt.

In the midst of my anguish, my oldest son, Jonathon, came to my defense. He grabbed the hands of his two younger brothers and stood them right before me. Then he put his little hand on my shoulder, pointed to his brothers, and said, "This is our mother. She is hurt real bad, but we must hug her."

After that, he swung both hands around my neck and kissed me on the forehead. In the sweetest, grown-up voice he could muster, he said, "Forgive them, Mother. They just don't understand." Joseph and Caleb followed the example set by their older brother, making physical contact. A hand on my leg and arm and shoulder—the relief was palpable. My soul was refreshed. It is one of the most memorable moments in my life.

> *This is our mother. She is hurt real bad, but we must hug her.*
> **—Jonathon Page**

Sweet acceptance, we all crave it. Many of us are desperate to obtain it. When someone is disfigured and scarred, the absence of acceptance intensifies the dejection. And then there is the problem of staring. Humans are drawn to that which is distinctive. If you think about it, we all have an urge to stare at anything that stands out to us. Not all stares are meant to be offensive. Sometimes people are simply curious and want to know your story. Realizing the normalcy of staring can help you deal with it better. Think about this. When a supermodel struts her stuff on the runway, we stare. If a celebrity were to show up at the restaurant your family was eating at, you would stare. Models and celebrities are comfortable in their own skin and feel they are worthy of your admiration.

When my family went to Golden Corral for dinner and people stared at Benjamin and me, why did it not feel the same way? Most likely it was because of how self-conscious I was about Ben. He was a two-year-old with severe facial burns. Dropped jaws and covered mouths did not communicate admiration, approval, or acceptance. Picking him up quickly, giving a rude stare back, or lashing out wasn't beneficial either.

Experience has taught me that when you have scarring or disfigurement, people respond according to the vibe they get about the way you feel about yourself. It takes time and healing to establish a healthy view of yourself after a traumatic experience. When I finally accepted my predicament and Ben's, it was easier for others to do the same.

Benjamin puts the charm in charmer. Every person who makes contact with him falls prey to his spell. Teachers, friends, and strangers alike fall in love with his irrepressible nature. So have I. He is everyone's boy, and even though he is willful, everyone is willing to bend the rules a bit for Ben's satisfaction. He can imitate anything and is mischievous in nature. The secret to managing Ben is to give him responsibility. He has a God-given gift to help.

One of the devastating results of the fire is that Benjamin is now mentally challenged and speech impaired. The blessing in disguise is that Benjamin is oblivious to rude remarks, jokes about his burns, or insensitive gaping. Since he can't process those things, I tend to take the teasing on. I would prefer that he had full mental capacity, but I was robbed of that choice by the fire. However, his cognitive level lessens the pain of teasing, and it is one less thing for him to deal with. His mental retardation, in effect, cushioned the blow.

I mastered the art of acceptance through the example set by Benjamin. In his eyes, everyone is on a level playing ground. You are a human, and he wants to love you. Everybody gets a chance. You have to prove yourself *un*worthy of his affection. I would watch in awe at how this child, whose intellectual functioning was supposedly below average, would handle the rudest people.

Ben always speaks first. You can be gawking, looking at him with disgust, but it doesn't matter. He will smile, raise his hand, wave it back and forth in a quick motion, and utter, "Hey." If you try to avert your eyes or ignore him, he will move into your space and repeat the process until you respond. Everyone responds. When you respond, he laughs a hearty laugh, and you cannot help but join in. What happens next is powerful. People forget the burns and begin to enjoy the person. How are they able to forget the severe burns that are plainly before them? Benjamin is not focused on them.

Injuries and scars do not define you. They are the result of an experience you had in your life. You are defined by the faith, character, and respect that guide you. I found that drawing attention to the inward man helps others see past the superficial scarring. Wouldn't it be nice to be like Ben—just to wave and make people laugh and connect with us? Not so easy for us who understand the full implication of blatant stares and turned-up noses. Still Ben had some basic principles working that will benefit us—no matter what our intellect is.

I modified Ben's example and drew three action steps that allow me to deal with staring, and it keeps me in the driver's seat every time. When someone stares, I make direct eye contact and take the initiative to speak. I don't try to judge the stare or the person; I make him prove his motives. Secondly, I smile. I am okay now, and I refuse to let others' pity take me backwards to the time of pain. Lastly, I share as little or as much as I want. I don't feel obligated to answer anyone's question. It's my story, and I stay in control.

I've watched Ben after he has engaged a person. Sometimes he will offer his ball for you to play with him. Sometimes Ben mimics you in an effort to communicate with you. Other times, he just stares at you and then walks away. He decides and remains the captain.

The downfall of any salesman, no matter what product or service he is promoting, is when he doesn't believe in the product he's selling. How can you sell me a cookie if you won't eat it? How can you promote a service you won't use? How can I demand acceptance from others when I don't accept myself? When you don't accept yourself, the chances of others doing so is drastically reduced. People will mirror your feelings. Your aura speaks volumes.

The work I do with The Amos House, Common Voices, the Phoenix Society, and as a speaker and author require travel to various conferences across the nation. It always amazes me that no matter where I am when I get off the elevator, people assume I am in charge. Before I even open my mouth, I get asked questions like, "Which state are you the district leader of?" or "What seminar are you teaching today?" or "What will you be speaking on?" and so forth. The assumption is that I am in authority and have something to offer.

I like that. I love to respond and say, "I'm just here to attend the conference with you." My posture, countenance, and smile leads people to believe that I am confident and comfortable with me.

A NOTE TO BURN SURVIVORS

Any person who has been disfigured, maimed, or scarred must first come to terms with it and accept himself. Make direct eye contact, hold your head high, smile, and walk with purpose. You are your first and most critical acceptance recruit.

Acceptance starts with the person accepting self, then accepting how others perceive him, then accepting how he is actually treated by those same people. It takes thick skin to deal with self-acceptance after a disfiguring burn trauma, but it can be done. I know!
—**Princella Lee-Bridges**, burn survivor; CEO and founder,
Bridges from Augusta, Inc.

I remember thinking when in the hospital, "I hope James will love me again the way he did before."

The thought of him rejecting me was terrifying. The thought of him with another woman sent me to the edge. The sad and glorious truth was, those were my thoughts alone. His thoughts were so far away it was astonishing. While I was worrying about being loved like before, he was thinking of ways to show a greater love. Accepting me wasn't even an issue for him.

When it comes to married couples, this acceptance issue can be misconstrued. I was assuming he was having a hard time accepting me because I was having a hard time accepting myself. He never said anything demeaning. He was always with me and encouraging me, yet my thoughts still laid charges at his door. This is something to beware of.

I remember a conversation with a close male friend during my freshman year in college. He was a medium height, decent-looking guy with an agreeable personality. We were alone at our work-study job on campus, having one of our intellectual conversations, as we liked to call them to humor ourselves. We would debate just about anything and prided ourselves on being honest about our feelings and opinions. He had a sharp, quick mind. I liked that.

The particular topic that day was his choice. He wanted to talk about dating. I wasn't clear if he was in a roundabout way trying to assess his opportunity with me or not. I hoped not; his height had already disqualified him. I dismissed the thought just as quickly as it came. I knew he didn't have feelings for me. No one had feelings for me. He started the conversation.

"The problem with females is that they assume all males are alike: they don't genuinely love; they just want sex."

I spoke up, saying, "True. Just like all males assume females feel the way you just described them. We lump everyone together in judgment, no matter if it is really just one thing shared in common. Reminds me of our great American justice system: guilty until proven innocent."

He laughed. "Point taken."

The conversation quickly took a personal turn. He looked me square in my eyes and asked, "Why don't you date?"

It was impossible for me to lie. I averted my eyes and answered, "I am afraid."

He looked me up and down as he responded in a low whisper, "Afraid of what? Goodness. You're beautiful."

That was the wrong thing to say. I was offended. I knew I was ugly and had accepted it a long time ago. I didn't want to play games.

"I thought we were going to be honest with each other."

His eyes registered greater shock. He jumped off the counter he was sitting on in front and sat on the counter right next to me. He placed his hands on each of my shoulders and turned me toward him before he spoke.

"You mean to tell me that you don't feel attractive? You don't think anyone wants to date you?"

He waited for my response. He had hit too close to home. All I could say was yes. He fell back on the counter and burst into a hysterical laugh. I didn't know what to think of him. I had exposed some real, private feelings. As he sat up, he dried his eyes and just looked at me for a moment. His eyes grew more serious than I had ever seen before.

"Tina. You are one of the most beautiful women on this campus. You have secret admirers a half-mile long who are at a loss on how to approach you. There is so much more to a real woman than looks."

I gave him a quick hug and said, "Thanks for the vote of confidence." He didn't respond; he just stared at me. I tried to ease the tension, break the silence, or do something to get the dialogue moving again.

I gave him a flirtatious smile and a playful wink and asked, "So, do you date?" Again he just stared at me. I couldn't read his expression. I began to feel a little uneasy.

I tried again from another angle. "So, what does your ideal date look like?"

He opened his mouth and closed it. Then he jumped off the table and stood in front of me. He placed his hands on the counter on either side of me and leaned in close to my face. He never broke eye contact, and his words were deliberate.

"My ideal date looks a lot like you." With that, he turned and slowly walked away.

All I could do was stare after him. I had not put two and two together. I was calloused by my self-esteem issues. In an effort to protect myself, I had not accepted him. As a matter of fact, a trivial thing such as his height had thrown him in my rejection pile. We have to make sure that the dish we hate to eat is not the dish we are serving to others.

I thought about his words for weeks after we talked. He had a valid point that is still viable today. We are so much more than a skinny waist, long hair, and a small nose. That's not much at all. There is a great deal more to an attractive person than that. Strength of character, integrity, personality, and compassion for others compose an attractive person.

After a traumatic event, altered surface looks cannot tarnish the beautiful person you can be inside. That is the part of you that you want to be accepted. Being accepted for a pretty face will phase out with time. Being accepted for the person you are inwardly never fades.

It is bad enough dealing with not being accepted. We have to make sure that because of our own misconceptions or low self-esteem, we are not discounting those who have open arms. Acceptance is often mirrored. If we accept ourselves, then others are more susceptible to accepting us. When life's sifter is used and the incredibly compassionate, warm-hearted people are finely mixed in your bowl of life, what about the junk on top that didn't go through? What about those with no grace or compassion? What about those who refuse to accept you as a soul worthy of respect and love, despite your outward appearance? Then what? Ignore them.

You cannot force people to accept you. Allot them space and time for growth, and meanwhile, enjoy those who do accept you. I don't mean to sound insensitive or callous. I know that rejection is painful. But, chasing acceptance, with no true chance of obtaining it, is more hurtful. A wounded leg is painful.

Wishing it wasn't so and hoping it will somehow just vanish is ridiculous. You have to get antibiotic cream, clean the wound, and cover it so it can heal. The same is true with rejection. It is not just going to go away. It has to be tended to, covered with love, and healed. I cover rejection by magnifying the acceptance that I have.

Prayer

Heavenly Father, I come to you in the name of Jesus.
I am so scared of rejection—especially from my husband.
Will everyone see me differently now?
Will people at the grocery store or in the mall look at me with disgust?
I do acknowledge your unconditional love.
Thank you for your acceptance.
You said that I was fearfully and wonderfully made.
Help me to discover the great gifts and talents that you have put
on the inside of me. Help me to accept myself as I am. I don't
want to be controlled by the thoughts and actions of others.
People are fickle. They can love you today and dislike you the next day.
Thank you for remaining the same.
I choose to see myself through your eyes—a person worthy of love.
In Jesus' name,
Amen.

Chapter 16

HOPE

From the ashes of my tragedy, a new hope has arisen.

T ime has a way of ushering hope to the forefront. When our basic needs have been addressed, hope is free to mature. When the threat of death is behind us and the threat of safety is not an issue, hope has an available conduit to flow freely through. Hope is a motivator to think and do the seemingly impossible. It is your greatest internal life coach. Hope grows your patience, endurance, and trust.

Paul said it best in the book of Romans: "Why should a man hope for that he already sees?" () Hope is most needed in the critical stage. It is the lifeline between despair and victory. It is needed not only for survival but also for living.

I reached for hope every time I had a surgery. I had so many surgeries, I lost count. Surgery was a challenging time for me. I didn't fear the procedure that was being done as much as I did the anesthesia. It was something about someone making me inhale a gas that knocked me unconscious and taking a drip that caused me to forget what happened that disturbed me to the core. Maybe I thought too deeply about it.

During surgery, I had no control or say in what was being done to me. The surgeons could do whatever they wanted. Somehow I managed to have the same person escort me to surgery for the duration of my first hospital stay. He was a short, younger gentleman with a kind and compassionate heart. He could sense my uneasiness and tried his best to ease my worry.

As he wheeled me through the hallways, on the service elevators, and to the operating prep room, we talked about my progress and how he knew I would make it. The peculiar thing about our conversations was that they ended the exact same way every time. His last words to me would be, "You are going to make it, baby. God is watching over you." I would say, "That's the hope."

Hope is God's means of transforming survival into living.
—**James R. Page Jr.**, beloved husband and father of my boys

What I was really saying every time I said those three words was this: I understood the seriousness of going under anesthesia. I also knew the complications that could arise from the procedures I was having. I was aware of my chances of survival. I had actually read the consent papers before I signed them. I was terrified, stressed, and in turmoil over my general predicament. But when I put all of my apprehensions on a scale together and balanced it against my desire to make it, hope was weightier. I was determined to believe it would all work out somehow, one surgery at a time.

I lived with my grandmother during my high school years. My grandmother ran a daycare center from her home. She was the favored daycare provider in the city. My grandmother was compassionate, creative, and had a gift of giving. We were concerned that the parents were taking advantage of her kindness. Whatever money she made, she gave most of it away. She loved surprising people with the very things they hoped for.

Her favorite time of year was Christmas. They were made for each other. The holiday fit her like a tailor-made suit. There wouldn't be walking room for the gifts spreading out well beyond the base of the tree. The basement would be full of gifts. The neighbors would be holding gifts. It was incredible. We got every last thing we hoped for. We never made a list, and she never asked. Somehow she knew exactly what we wanted. I was in junior high school before I caught on to what she was doing.

Personally, I felt like she didn't owe me anything.

I caught the principle. The more I put in, the greater the reward. That principle is relevant to the hope we have as well. As a matter of fact, your hope is only as strong as the actions you take to support it. I hoped with all my heart that I would be able to walk again. To support that hope, I had to move my leg up and down when the therapist told me to. I hoped with all my might to use my hands. I couldn't hold them in my lap and make that hope a reality. I had to endure the pain it took to get them moving. Occasionally, hope will cause you to travel down a road called pain. In order to cross and not turn back, think of pain as a bridge to desire. It is the pathway that will allow you to bypass defeat.

Hope has the power to produce something from nothing and unlatches the seal on opportunity. I was confined to a bed with the stench of death, devastation, and grief swirling around me. When everything that could happen wrong has happened and it appears to be all over for you, hope focuses your eyes on fresh chances. Hope is still available when everything else is gone.

In the midst of that setting, I thought about James and the kids. I had to recover for them. I felt that we could start over again. A new hope was birthed from the realization that we were alive; there was still a life available for us. When you need motivation to keep going in the face of a tedious journey, hope is your greatest motivator. If there is a desired prize in mind, you will go for it. Hope sets that prize within arm's length right before you. Never lose hope. A great deal is lost in that treasure chest. Vitality is nestled in hope, and possibilities are endless on the heels of hope.

When we abandon hope, we deny God his chance to work for us. We also shut the door of opportunity and lock it. The absence of hope is the abandonment of forward progress. If I had not acted on the hope of using my hands again, they would be mangled, twisted, and of no use unto this day. It would have produced a domino effect. I could have then lost my hope to walk and, eventually, my hope to live.

Hope is an internal lamp that sheds light on the deeper desires of your heart. It is an outward manifestation of "the why" in a person's life. There are many people at this moment in a critical stage on ICU burn units around the world. I would dare to say that ninety-five percent of them hope they live. It's the "why they hope to live" that will keep that hope breathing. When the "why" cannot be answered, hope has less chance of survival and is likely to die an untimely death.

Knowing why is empowering. It wasn't enough for me just to hope to live while I lay in bed with my body wracked in pain, not knowing what my quality of life would be. The formidable question that I had to answer was why? Live for what? Not having an answer for that question would have set my hope on a precarious slope. I wanted to live. I wanted to be with my husband and children. I wanted it with every fiber of my being; therefore, my hope was strong as steel.

I endured many difficult situations because of that deep desire in my heart. Where a man's heart is, there his treasure will be also (). That is one of the truest statements I have ever read in the Bible. Whatever you value personally, your heart will support that. When your heart is in a thing, you will cherish and protect it furiously. Sometimes "whys" are not so easy to unearth. When there seems not to be a reason for hope, what do you do then?

For an extended period of time, I provided peer support for a patient who was in a fire with his wife and five children. He was severely burned, his wife had multiple injuries, and he had lost all five of his kids. I talked with him almost every day.

At my initial visit with him, his first question was, "Why did I live?"

I took my time, looked him directly in the eye, and answered as honestly as I could: "I don't know."

That drew a chuckle from him, despite the horridness of the moment. He later revealed that he thought I would come up with some superficial reason, like there must be a purpose and so on. The second question he asked gave me greater pause, "Why should I live?" The hardness in his eyes pinned me to my seat. Thoughts of my overwhelming reason to desire life flooded my mind: my children and my husband. Every hope I had somehow entangled itself within my family.

This, however, was not applicable for him. This man had lost all five of his children in one tragic event. His wife had suffered multiple injuries, would not speak to him, and was threatening to leave him. I was temporarily stumped. Still, I was desperate to extend to this man some kind of hope to latch on to. Anything. The seriousness of the moment drew sweat beads down my back. I turned slightly and stroked the keloid on the right side of my neck, a common gesture for me when I am in serious thought.

I told him I had an assignment for him. His eyebrows arched; he was clearly confused by my response. I continued, "I will think more on your question, and I promise to answer it tomorrow. But I want you to think about a question and answer it tomorrow. Why should you *not* live?"

His eyes softened. I could see the internal battle working across his face.

Finally he said, "Sounds fair to me."

We began to talk about other things, his family in Chicago, his favorite restaurant, and so on. I was trying to distract him from despair, the ever-lurking scavenger of trauma patients. He thanked me for the visit and made me promise to come back the next day. I ensured him I would if he would promise to be here also. He laughed again and said that I could count on it.

The next day I came in, eager to hear his answer. He was animated and started talking before I even got seated.

"Okay, Mrs. Page. I want to live. I can't think of a real reason not to. Now, why should I live?"

I looked at him and a slight smile formed on my face. I rested my chin in the palm of my hand and said, "You have already answered the question yourself. You should live because you want to and you can't think of a good reason not to."

A huge smile spread across his face as tears gently released themselves. "Thanks" is all he could manage to say.

We eventually became good friends, and our visits were mainly centered on keeping that hope alive. Hope is the most potent weapon in your arsenal when combating despair. It is the reason we keep looking and moving forward. Hope is a chaser. It pursues its desire with passion. Hope is the bridge between survival and desire.

Hope should not be related only to one's desire to live. Its reach is much broader, and it has vast depths. Neither is hope limited to a particular number. You can hope for one thing or fifteen things. It doesn't matter. Our personal desires vary greatly. The end goal of hope is fulfillment.

Nothing could compare to the jubilation I felt when I was finally able to walk again. That jubilation doubled when I was able to use my hands and regained my independence. I felt like I was flying above the clouds. All of the simple things we take for granted in life became big deals to me: walking, sitting, talking, eating, holding, seeing, cooking, cleaning, and the list did not stop. It was as if I was starting life from the beginning, experiencing it new for the first time. All because of a fulfilled hope, the hope to make it through.

King Solomon said in the book of Proverbs, "Hope deferred makes the heart sick but when the desire comes it is a tree of life" (13:12). That is one of many scriptures that was fulfilled in my life. It made all the pain, fear, and endurance worth it.

Hope, however, does not go unchallenged. Fatigue, pain, and a whole assortment of difficulties all threaten to strip us of our most precious desires. Have you ever hoped for something so long and so strongly, only to let fatigue win, causing you to give up on that desire? It happens to the best of us. When hope has been strangled by the fallacies of the day and you say within yourself, *I don't care* or *I give up*, don't despair. Let it rest for a night or two and then pick that hope back up again. It is a blessing that hope can be renewed.

Prayer

Heavenly Father, I come to you in the name of Jesus.

Thank you for being with me so far.

This has been a difficult time for me and my family.

My hope is that everything will turn out all right.

I'm trying not to fret but to stay hopeful.

I know hope will not make me ashamed.

There are many things I want to see happen,

but a few are a must for me.

I want to use my hands again.

Please give me strength to endure the therapy.

I want to walk and be independent again.

I need patience to wait for it to happen.

Thank you for hearing me. My hope is in you.

In Jesus' name,

Amen.

Chapter 17

SOCIAL RE-ENTRY

We may not be able to dictate the hand we get in life,
but we still have a powerful weapon: choice.

One of our first outings as a family after the fire was to my favorite mall in Houston, Baybrook Mall. We all clambered into "white lightning," our white Plymouth Voyager van, and headed south to do my favorite thing in the world: shop. I was so excited. I was finally at a point where walking did not fatigue me.

Our first destination, of course, was Game Stop. Jonathon, Joseph, and Caleb scurried in to find games for their play station while Benjamin, Daniel, my husband, and I sat on a nearby bench and enjoyed fresh Cinnabon rolls. Benjamin was still wearing his black pressure garments, which covered his face, arms, and hands. I had on brown pressure garments that covered my hands, arms, and upper torso.

From our point of view, the setting was a refreshing return to normalcy for us. However, the looks on the faces of others within the mall challenged that feeling of normalcy. The stares were pointed, but the exaggerated effort not to look at us was even more offensive. The general response of the shoppers suggested we were trespassing at this mall. What was wrong with our family? Was there a special mall for burn survivors that I wasn't aware of? Didn't they realize that we had survived a traumatic ordeal and were all the stronger for it? Did we simply not fit into this social setting because of our misfortune? God forbid.

We were different. Difference beckons attention. The interesting thing is that all of us are different. It's just that internal differences are not as visible as physical ones. Can you imagine a world where our insides are turned out? Can you imagine the stares and shuns we would give each other? Thank God for his wisdom to keep our insides hidden.

The response of the mall shoppers put a temporary damper on the excitement and exhilaration I was feeling about being out as a family together. Then I came to myself. We may not be able to dictate the hand we get in life, but we still have a powerful weapon: choice. It was not up to the shoppers to determine if we would enjoy ourselves. It was up to us. My choice was to ignore them and continue on with the plan to shop.

I knew the children would follow our lead. My enthusiasm returned with a vengeance. My husband set a budget; I mapped a plan; and the show was back on the road. Before I knew it, we were in a world of our own, laughing, eating, and having a wonderful time. The few people who ventured into our world, inquiring about what happened, didn't bother me at all. In fact, I was touched by their compassion and willingness to help if they could. From that point on, I found myself driven to prove my normalcy and independence. I was still going through intense therapy and was in and out of splints on my hands. But I had mastered the art of improvising, which allowed me to do most of what I wanted.

A NOTE TO BURN SURVIVORS

Don't use your burn injury as a crutch or as a reason to feel inferior to others. Our mindset and contribution to society is what sets us apart. Set the standard for yourself as to who you want to be and what purpose you want to accomplish. Scars won't prohibit you from accomplishment—unless you allow it. Neither can disfigurement or amputation. It may take some improvising and a bit of creativity, but your goals can still be accomplished.

When I went to PTO meetings, I didn't want the parents treating me differently because of what I went through. Empathy is one thing, but pity was another. When people pity you, their expectations of you are low. They don't expect much of you, so they don't grant much opportunity for you either.

I still remember the faces of the parents when I came to the PTO general meeting at the first elementary school Joseph and Caleb attended. I had Benjamin with me, with his blue suction machine in tow. It was obvious that they pitied us. I was given special treatment. A parent offered me a seat in the front row, right where I wanted to be. Another parent brought Benjamin and me snacks and drinks. Their eyes hinted that they were curious about our story. No one wanted to ask, though, for fear of offending us.

The meeting began and progressed to the point where it was time to elect new members for the PTO board. The organization had just switched over from being a PTA to a PTO and wanted a fresh start. All slots were open, and you were free to nominate yourself. The lady who conducted the meeting spoke in a proud voice, "We are now taking nominations for president."

Before anyone could blink, my hand was up. She looked at me startled, "Yes ma'am?" I stood and cleared my throat.

"I would like to nominate myself for president."

Everyone seemed paralyzed. I didn't know if they thought I had a speech impediment or what the problem was. The meeting conductor recovered herself after a while.

"Okay. Are there any more nominations for president?"

No one moved. As a matter of fact, everyone was still looking at me. I was totally amused. I became the president of the PTO my first year with kids in public school. I received an award that year for establishing new programs that improved the overall attendance and behavior of the student body, each at its highest mark since the school had been in existence. I was also honored for taking care of the emergency needs of the teachers.

Justina speaking at the World Burn Congress in New York

The point is this: I was re-entering a world where I was used to functioning. My outward appearance was deceiving. I challenge all of you to re-enter your social settings with boldness and dignity. Take it a step further and try something new. Stretch your courage. You will be pleased with the satisfaction you get from doing so.

> *Throughout my post-burn high school experience, I never once used my being burned as a crutch, because firstly, I wanted, at all costs, to avoid a situation where my good grades would be ascribed to my situation. I have to say that, contrary to what I expected, I was quite well received by the staff and students of the school On the whole, I would say that rejoining society once more has taken a bit of courage on my part.*
> —**Kechi Ijeoma**, Nigerian plane crash survivor

As much as I hate to admit it, I am a Wal-Mart addict. It's a shopaholic's dream world, especially if your money is limited. The family had spent a full day out, and as we were heading home, I asked my husband if he would mind stopping by Wal-Mart. If you don't want the honest truth, it is not advisable to ask my husband. His answer was quick: no. I continued pressing my case.

"But we need trash bags and some other things."

He was not deterred. "It is nine o'clock at night, and the kids need to get home and so do you."

My pouting began in full force. "I feel fine and can finally do something on my own. I just want to have a few more minutes of freedom."

He compromised. "Okay, but I am not going in."

I was shocked. "But how am I going to get the things I need with the splints on?"

He threw my words back at me, "You can finally do something on your own, right?"

I was instantly angry. Now I had to prove myself to him of all people. I told him I would be just fine and that Jonathon, Joseph, and Caleb could help me. I maneuvered my way out of the front seat and told the boys to follow. My pace was slow and steady, yet I noticed the boys were drifting farther and farther back. I glanced over my shoulder and called for them to keep up. The gap between me and them was widening.

I whirled around and asked them in a sarcastic voice, "Is something wrong? Is it hard to keep up with me as fast as I am?" It was as if they were intentionally trying to keep a yard's distance between us.

The looks on their faces weren't quite right. Caleb looked as if he had seen a ghost. Jonathon looked totally disturbed. And Joseph—his father's son both in mind and spirit—looked oblivious to everything, lost in his own world. I couldn't take it any longer.

"What is the problem?" I asked in an irritated voice.

Caleb immediately covered his eyes. Jonathon opened his mouth to speak, but the audible words were frozen. Joseph looked me directly in my eyes and said in a matter of fact tone, "Well, actually, Mom, your behind is showing."

I was mortified. In my determination to get out of the car on my own, my skirt and slip had gotten tangled and caught in the waist band, and I was baring my underwear to the unfortunate Wal-Mart shoppers behind me.

Before I could get my composure, the flow of tears began. Jonathon immediately hugged me and said, "I'm sorry, Mother."

Caleb wasn't sure what to do. And Joseph—like father, like son—looked as if he didn't understand what the problem was. I told them that I was going to turn around and asked if they would please pull my skirt down. Jonathon and Joseph nodded their heads yes, but Caleb was having no part in it. They covered my shame, and, of course, my desire to shop had vanished. We went straight to the car, got in, and rode home in complete silence.

My husband knew something was wrong by the silent flow of tears slipping down my face but wisely decided to ask me in private when we got home. It was two weeks before humiliation had run its full course and I had any desire to make social appearances. Talk about your self-esteem taking a beating.

I did, however, recover and discovered something about myself. I didn't want a middle road. I wanted complete independence or complete dependence. I wanted to put the sock on and pull it all the way up. If I could only just put it on my foot, I would rather you put it on and pull it up. I didn't like me putting it on and you pulling it up. That had to change—especially if I wanted to re-enter my social settings fully. I found I was only participating on levels where I had regained full control. But I was robbing myself of so many activities and outings that I could still enjoy with a little assistance. I was always the helper, but the tables had turned. I had to learn to become comfortable with receiving help—even in public.

I have made enormous strides since my burn injury, but I still have small limitations. I still need help cutting my steak occasionally. I was comfortable asking my husband and family. But when I went on business trips, I felt shy about asking. I would order food that I could eat without any assistance. At one meeting I had at a steakhouse here in Houston, however, steak was the only meat on the menu. I was forced to ask for help. Honestly, it wasn't that bad. It turned out to be a great icebreaker. Now, I am even more comfortable with me, limitations and all.

A common mistake I have seen among burn survivors is the tendency to confine themselves to a small box where they feel most accepted. Generally, that will only include family and burn staff, the ones they see as caring and understanding. My challenge to burn survivors is to return to the world you love—no matter what physical damages you have sustained. Don't let the world shut you out. Break the door down if you have to, and live.

I was married at the time of my accident. Prior to my accident, I enjoyed dinners with my husband, walks in the park, trips, and romantic evenings. Anyone close to me knows that I love surprising people. I have been accused of being extravagant in my methods, but I am rewarded by the sheer shock and joy on the face of the recipient. I refused to let my physical alterations shut me out from my social enjoyment. Till this day, my husband and I enjoy our dates as often as opportunity presents itself. And my surprises are getting more sophisticated as the years pass. Why would I deny myself that because someone else feels uneasy about my looks? The world is a big place. There is room for all of us here.

There are three proven concepts that I have used to transition smoothly back into the social settings I enjoy. The first is education. Before our fire, I had never met a burn survivor in my life. I had no idea what a first- or second- or third-degree burn was. I had never heard of skin grafting and pressure garments. I was uninformed.

Many of the people staring at you or shying away from you are the same way. The braces, splints, and miscellaneous contraptions can be a little frightening to a person who knows nothing about what's going on. They find themselves in a position where they don't know what to say or do.

This is especially true of children. A few years after the fire, I went to Benjamin's school to volunteer on picture day. I knew that Benjamin was afraid of lights and that the big camera flash might traumatize him. He related all big lights to the surgery room where he went in lying on a gurney with a cascade of big lights above him, only to wake up groggy and in pain. My duty was to keep the class in line and assist the students up the steps to the stage for their portrait to be taken as their names were called. The children had name tags on so I wouldn't send Bob up when it was Sue's turn. I was monitoring a first grade class when Shanae stepped up and looked at me, cow-eyed with a dropped jaw.

Finally, she said in a loud and terrified voice, "What happened to you?"

I turned to her, matching her stance and voice, and said, "I was burned."

She threw her hand over her mouth and said, "Really?"

"Really. Would you like to see?"

She nodded her head up and down vigorously, and her eyes widened another inch. I pulled my sweater sleeve up and allowed her to feel the grafts on my arm as I briefly explained what had happened and a little about third-degree burns and skin grafting. Other kids in the line began to gather around and join my impromptu lesson about burns.

We were interrupted by the photographer calling Shanae's name. I reached for her hand with my right hand, the one with partially amputated fingers. She hesitated, grabbed my hand tenderly, and whispered, "Does it hurt? I don't want to hurt you."

It was a teachable moment. Look at the compassion and acceptance a little education produced. I could have cowered at her blatant question and thought, *I will never volunteer at the elementary school again.* But I understood the reality of the situation. The little girl was just being honest; she had no idea what had happened, and she wanted to know. It was also true that my appearance was slightly different from the other adult volunteers there.

As I pondered on that situation later that evening, a light bulb went on. Many adults are in the same predicament. They are clueless and want to know. However, to call out "What happened to you?" as an adult is not socially acceptable.

From that experience, I decided to become an educator and bridge builder. Instead of becoming uncomfortable or offended, I strive to bridge the gap between my story and others' lack of understanding. I want them to be educated about burn injuries.

The second re-entry concept I mastered was not to limit myself. It is so easy for us who have been through a traumatic experience to tell ourselves that life will never be the same again. Technically, that may be true, but in theory, it is faulty. What we are really saying is that the enjoyment and fulfillment we had in life will be no more. I say that's not necessarily so. We are capable of so much more than we attempt. Our mind is often our worst stumbling block. My encouragement to you is not to knock it until you try it. It doesn't matter what your physical state is; for the most part, when there is a will, there is a way.

When we lived in California, there was a traveling circus called "The Flying Souls." They had some of the best circus performers I had ever seen in my life.

One day they advertised that they were going to have auditions for children who wanted to perform as trapeze artists. My older sister was elated. She was an excellent acrobat and had great athletic ability. She wanted my younger sister and me to try out with her. We were not as talented as she was, but we had considerable acrobatic and athletic skills as well.

We agreed to try out with her, and our mother took us to the audition. Even with my tendency to think things over, there was one thing I failed to consider. I was afraid of heights. We were in line when the realization dawned on me.

Kelly went right up the rope ladder with her spotter, following his instructions to a tee. She was a natural. Kelly was accepted on the team before she even got back down the ladder. I was next. My back was perspiring so heavily that they had to get paper towels to wipe me off. Before I approached the ladder, I contemplated turning around and never coming back. But I had promised Kelly I would try. I decided then and there that the least I could do was try.

That's the decision many of us burn survivors face when re-entering social settings after our hospital stays. It can be scary and uncomfortable to mingle within your social circle again, but you have to try. Did I become a renowned young trapeze artist? No. Kelly did. As a matter of fact, I never even touched the horizontal bar. But I did climb as far as I could go, and I was proud of that. I didn't let fear limit me. When you go as far as you know you can go, you will be proud of yourself as well.

The third concept for re-entering society, and perhaps the most important, is being comfortable with being yourself. It is empowering to be at peace with who you are right now. I stopped trying to be something I wasn't just to fit in. That technique was driven by an overwhelming desire to be accepted. Being accepted by many had a way of stroking my ego and deceiving me into believing I was important. The funny thing is that it doesn't take an assembly of people to establish that. God has confirmed my importance by creating me and showering me with the many gifts and talents I have. My place on this earth is unique. So is yours.

Have you ever considered the fact that there are billions of people on the face of the earth, and not one of us has the same fingerprints? Snowflakes fall from one side of the universe to the other, and no two of them are identical. No two minds and no two hearts are the same either. So why do we try to change ourselves to be more like another person? It's a futile effort. Nature is against that, and God has not designed it to be so. What we need is support and encouragement to be who we are. I may not look like you or do it like you, but as long as I get the job done, I am not inferior to you

The truth is this, when you equip the burn survivor under your care with all the love, warmth, and acceptance that you can provide, and give all the positive reinforcement that you know how to, he goes out into society knowing that, while he may look different and do things differently due to some limitations caused by his injuries, he is in no way inferior to anyone else.

–**EJ**, Amos House volunteer and mother of sole Nigerian plane crash survivor

Amos House of Faith Gala 2010

We moved from California back to Missouri at the beginning of my fourth grade year. The fads and styles in LA were years ahead of the Midwest. We came back with our noses pierced, strange clothing, and stranger ideas. The kids in the neighborhood weren't allowed to socialize with us.

There was a girl my age who lived across the street and two houses over. She came from a well-rounded home: mother, father, and three siblings. My household was the epitome of dysfunction. The girl and I would sneak down to the bottom of the street and talk. We found each other's lives interesting.

One day we got caught. It was a huge mess. Arguments broke out between the two families. We stood in the middle of the chaos, crying.

Finally I asked, "Why can't we play together? We live on the same street."

Shame filled the faces of our parents and siblings. From that point on, we were allowed to be friends. Our families eventually became close. We called each other cousins.

June became my first true and best friend. We were so close and did so many things together that even when we were alone, people spoke and said, "Hi, Tina. Hi, June."

We even went to college together, and she was the maid of honor in my wedding. All of that would never have been if I were not allowed re-entry into the neighborhood. At nine years old, I had a run-in with social re-entry. I had lived on that same block before with no problems. But when I went to LA and came back a different person, it was hard for others to accept me, even though I was the same person I was before I left.

It is similar for burn survivors who have experienced physical impairment. When you get released from the hospital back to the environment you came from, some people will not want to accept you simply because of the external differences. You cannot force them to do so. What I did at age nine and what I did again at age thirty-one after I was burned was to help others look past the differences that seemingly separated us. As a burn survivor, I have conquered looking past my burns, scars, and amputation, but I needed time to do so. Others may need time as well.

Prayer

Heavenly Father, I come to you in the name of Jesus.
There is nothing like being free.
I want to live again, even more fully and happier than before.
Society wants to shut me out because of my burns.
Give me strength, I pray, to press forward.
I don't want to feel ashamed about my appearance.
I don't want to stop enjoying the things I like to do
because someone else is uncomfortable with me being around.
Help my kids not react to the prejudice that sometimes occurs.
Give us all strength as a family to be comfortable in our own skin.
Help me not to push people away or miss opportunities
because of what I feel about myself.
Thank you for accepting me in the family of God, where it doesn't
matter what my outward appearance is. I am encouraged to move on.
In Jesus' name,
Amen.

Chapter 18

PURPOSE

I was no longer a burn victim but a bona fide survivor.
I began to feel a sense of purpose.

hrough much prayer, support, and the unconditional love of family, friends, and church family, I began to transcend my circumstances. I was no longer a burn victim but a bona fide survivor. I began to feel a sense of purpose. My faith was intact, and I began to look at the needs of others, the men, women, and children who were unfortunately experiencing the same depth of pain, heartache, despair, and anger as I had.

I had stumbled upon purpose. Purpose is powerful. It is the warring faction that combats the "Why me?" syndrome. It disarms and conquers confusion every time. When you know what you are destined for, you can get to the business of making it happen.

My purpose is to impart faith, strength, and hope to those who are in desperate need of it. Many families will be blessed as a result. God has given every man a set of gifts and talents to be used for his glory and honor. Our experiences provide a platform for these gifts to come forward and be fine-tuned for that specific purpose.

Purpose is one of mankind's lifelong pursuits, mainly because our fulfillment is hidden in it. Life's experiences are a stairwell to purpose. It will get you there sooner or later. Many of us begin at an early age in our endeavor to discover purpose. Purpose prods us to ask the "whys" in our life. Not all whys are easy to answer. Some things in life just don't make sense. There are sometimes no answers to the elusive whys. I am glad that the answer to why is not the key to purpose. There is not a direct correlation.

Many patients that I have supported on the burn unit have asked me the whys of their life. I am quick to tell them that I have not been able to answer all the whys in my own life. The whys in other people's lives are not for me to answer. The only one who knows all the whys is God. And I do know that sometimes he chooses not to share his reasons. *Why* rarely makes sense of the trouble we have endured. On the other hand, purpose usually answers the question well. Don't let an unanswered why distract you from getting to purpose.

I can safely say that no burn survivor would chose to show up one day on a bed in a burn unit. Neither did we choose the surgeries, amputations, and painful therapy that followed. But we found ourselves in that place and now have that experience under our belts. Purpose definitely can be extracted from our journey.

The big achievements that are visible to man are not the only signs of purpose playing out in your life. Not every burn survivor will build a foundation, write a book, or become a peer supporter. Some will never see or speak to another burn survivor again in their lives.

Sometimes we strive to be bigger and better, and it is a continual burden on our shoulders. That desire is not equivalent to purpose. Purpose is not burdensome. Bigger and better is not necessarily your purpose. Purpose is not limited to questions of grandeur; purpose is natural and simple. It could be learning to be kinder or more appreciative after the trauma. Your journey could have drawn you and your family closer together.

Burn survivors have shared stories about how they aren't as materialistic as before and how they've been spending more quality time with their children. No one wants to experience a trauma, but when a trauma produces these types of results, the sacrifices can seem far less daunting.

> *I work because I want to—not because I have to. Patients don't choose to come to us, but we choose to work for them.*
> —**Stephanice Stephan**, RN, BSN, clinical manager,
> John S. Dunn Sr. Burn Center

For you to fulfill your purpose, it is not necessary for the world to know about what you are doing. There are millions of people successfully doing what God has chosen them to do, yet they are people the world will never know.

As soon as I was well enough to do so, I sat in a chair outside of my hospital room for the greater part of the day. I was serving an exceptional purpose that not even the nurses, doctors, or visitors knew about. I had already been through the excruciating tank experiences and had moved on to the shower room.

The burn unit was a revolving door. Someone new was always coming in. I would sit in the hall, pray, and smile at the newcomers who were on their way to the tank. Occasionally, I would squeeze a hand or talk if someone wanted to. My purpose was to lower the stress and help ease the anxiety of those who were having that horrific scrubbing experience. I had been in their shoes. I knew how much a smile or kind words meant to me. My heart was filled with compassion for their plight. I didn't need a medal or a standing ovation for what I was doing. It was purpose, and the reward was fulfilling it.

My siblings and I were serious competitors. Our world revolved around the blue ribbon, gold medal, or first place trophy. Those awards were our pride and joy. I remember the first time I competed when my standing in the competition meant nothing to me, when I didn't even have me in mind. I competed to fulfill a purpose.

It was my senior year in high school and the last track meet for the year. I ran the quarter and the mile relay, but my popularity was due to my ability in the field events: high jump, long jump, and in particular, the triple jump. I was one of the best in the city, every competitor's marked rival. My accomplishments circulated throughout the city in newspapers and by word of mouth. If you could beat me, you were good.

There was a sophomore from another school who was good also. It was obvious she was going to become the next up-and-coming triple jump star. She had one problem. She was intimidated by me. She had never been able to beat me. In a triple jump competition, you get three jumps, and the judges take the best of the three as your record jump. We had jumped the first two. I was winning so far and feeling pretty good about it until I saw her face. I could tell she wanted nothing more than to beat me before I left the high school competition arena.

It may sound crazy, but I liked what I saw, and I wanted her to win too. I walked past the other jumpers, caught her by the shoulders, and greeted her. Then I asked her a question, "Do you want to know how to beat me?" She laughed. She wasn't shocked by my action. I had a pretty bad reputation. No one knew what I was going to do next. My nickname was "Crazy T," if that gives you any idea. This kid had two more years of competing left. What better way to start the next school year than by having confidence backed by beating the reigning triple jump star? As far as I was concerned, this would be my last jump ever. I wasn't planning on pursuing track in college. It was study time for me. I wanted to be an electrical engineer. I let my hands drop to my side and moved closer to her,

"I'm serious. I know you want to beat me."

She smiled. "Of course I do."

I smiled back and said, "Okay, start with this. Tell yourself you can. You are better than me."

She really did have better technique than I did. I was just more confident and arrogant. I gave her the best advice I could think of. I had come to the track meet with a purpose to win gold in all four competitions and leave the sport with a bang.

My purpose changed, however, when I saw how valuable that gold would be to her. I intuitively understood my glory would fade quickly, so why not help hers blossom? She won that competition. We took a picture together with the first place metal hanging between us. I didn't have the gold, but the silver I won that day was more fulfilling than all the gold I've won in my entire athletic career.

There is a stark difference between my purpose and God's. God's purpose for you is not selfish in nature. If the only one who benefits from what you do is you, you are definitely doing your own thing. Purpose involves others. Even if your purpose is to increase your self-esteem, that goal still affects others. When your self-esteem is healthy, your relationships are healthy. Selfish ambition is a sure way to distract you from your purpose.

When we were in high school, all the junior year students were given a career ability test. The test was designed to tell you what career path would be best for you, based on your academic skill and personality. The two major results were "Career Fields Compatible with Skills" and "Career Fields Compatible with Personality." The top three careers for me on the personality side were education, sociology, and culinary arts. I didn't need a test to tell me that. I had wanted to be a teacher all my life, loved working with and understanding the thought processes of people, and had been cooking full meals for my grandmother since I was eight.

The skill side was interesting: engineer, inventor, scientist. That made sense also being that my strengths were math and science. What I focused on was the projected annual salaries for each of these career paths. I wanted to be a teacher, but I was smart enough to be an engineer. The engineering salary ran a ring around the teacher's salary, so on to engineering school I went. However, I had no passion for it, nor even a good understanding of what engineers do. I was motivated by the money. I wish someone had had the wisdom to counsel me about purpose.

I studied electrical engineering for four years, only to teach in a private Christian school and then homeschool my own children for ten years. I have never worked an engineering job in my life. I never regretted that choice either.

My heart was drawn to my purpose. I feel my career as an engineer would have seriously lacked purpose. Life without purpose is a life with little value. It lacks passion and vitality. Purpose is the meat in life's sandwich.

> *If your purpose is to save lives, one of the actions required can be to go into a burning building. There are risks, but the rewards come in the form of lives saved. The purpose of a fireman's life is to save lives.*
> —**Chief Rick Flanagan**, Houston Fire Department

You cannot find purpose or achieve it looking backwards. "What if" scenarios are futile. They don't change your reality. I have run them around in my head long enough to know. What if I had put batteries in the smoke detector and the fire had not happened? Would I be working with burn survivors now? Would I have been able to continue teaching the kids?

In reality, it doesn't matter. That "what if" would only serve to make me despise the purpose I can see now. And every "what if" I construct in my mind can be complicated by a counter "what if," causing a greater disturbance and total confusion. What if my husband had not been able to get any of us out? Here's the catch: that didn't happen.

Try to stick to the basics when it comes to purpose. This is what happened, and this is what I am doing now. You may have been put on the earth to accomplish one thing. Or, perhaps you have a multitude of purposes. The important thing is to fulfill the work you are given. When you fulfill your purpose, others are blessed. When others fulfill their purposes, I am blessed. Whatever your purpose is, do it with conviction, and give it your best. Half-hearted attempts won't do.

Anyone who knows me at all knows this one thing about me when it comes to projects or missions: either I'm in or I'm out. I'm with you, or I'm not. It works better that way. According to the writer of the book of Ecclesiastes, there is a time and season for every purpose under the sun (). That lets me know that purposes pass and change. Don't get bogged down thinking about your purpose. If you don't find it, it will find you. When it does, take care of business.

I've found my purpose in telling my story and volunteering with the burn community. In my time spent with these hurting people, I have witnessed that fire is not discriminatory. I have seen CEOs of major corporate businesses in a room on the burn unit next to a homeless person. I have seen great grandmothers and infants, as well as those from varied racial backgrounds, genders, sizes, political orientations, and religious views—all brought to common ground through the tragedy of fire. Chance is the common denominator. The sobering reality is we don't know what a day may bring. Even a day that is illuminated with the most resplendent sunshine can become an atrocious storm. Now what? I say let's enjoy sunshine while we have it, and let's have a backup plan for the storm that is likely to come. After the storm passes, look around you. What have you learned? How can you apply it? Remember, your experiences, your purpose, can bring help, hope, and healing to those still struggling.

After Burns Club Galveston

*After Burns Club at
Ronald McDonald House*

*After Burns Club Galveston
Topic: Teasing*

*After Burns Club Galveston
Topic: Staring*

*After Burns Club Galveston
Toilet Paper Idol*

*After Burns Club Galveston
Volunteers*

Prayer

Heavenly Father, I come to you in the name of Jesus.

Lord, thank you for making me feel alive—not just
with breath and a functioning mind, but with purpose.

I feel so much purpose for my life.

Thank you for giving me the privilege of helping others.

Help me be sensitive to the times and seasons in my life.

Give me strength to change when they do.

Things don't always stay the same. I have learned that the hard way.

Bless the many burn survivors I see on a weekly basis
with an understanding of your purpose.

There is life in that. Help me not to compare myself to anyone.

You said that to do so is not wise.

I trust you to fulfill your total will in my life.

In Jesus' name,

Amen.

Chapter 19

TRIUMPH

So how does one transcend difficult circumstances—
even rising above or going beyond them?

T
he transformation from burn victim to burn survivor is initiated when the victim is able to use his experience as a foundation and build on it. I have been blessed to establish and build upon a solid foundation. I know and understand the immeasurable benefit that love and support plays in a post-burn support environment. I have experienced chaos metamorphosing itself into peace, pain bearing the fruit of joy, and weakness making way for strength. Out of all the many privileges and opportunities that I have been able to achieve, my greatest accomplishment is my sanity. The peace and stability that I have in Christ supersedes every accolade.

A person who triumphs is a person who has won the battle—a battle against an enemy that would have them in a compromised place. We should not try to do this alone. We are not islands. It takes people within and without the burn community to catapult us to a triumphant arena.

I have enjoyed my interaction with the burn community, which is made up of so many special people, each having a specific purpose. There is the medical community, including, surgeons, doctors, nurses, techs, therapists, social workers, nutritionist, chaplaincy service, and volunteers, all of whom have one-on-one contact with the patients, all ensuring that physical health is restored. The fire department, including firemen, arson investigators, and EMS teams, also play a crucial role, working on either side of the fence, trying to protect you from tragedy or trying to get you help when the unthinkable happens.

Justina Page on the John S. Dunn Sr. Burn Unit

Then there are burn-support organizations, foundations, charities, and support groups, all established to ensure that the quality of life of the burn survivor is good and his emotional health is stable. Last but not least are the burn survivors themselves, which includes the patients, the caregivers, and their family members. It is a painful initiation to endure, but it wasn't an initiation by choice.

I have learned the closeness of the burn survivor community is an integral part of the journey of healing. This special group includes the survivors, family, friends, and the medical community. It is a daunting experience to endure this type of injury, yet there is solace in the fact that nobody has to go through it alone.
—**Jerry Donovan**, creative consultant

Triumph does not have a universal measure. It is tailor made for the person obtaining it. The one thing in common for everyone who experiences triumph is that the enemy that was conquering you is now being conquered by you. After a long, painful, scary battle, nothing is sweeter than triumph, trampling over your tragedy as you hold your head up with purpose and pride. How much sweeter the victory is when your triumph turns into a vehicle to help others ride to assurance and safety.

So how does one transcend difficult circumstances—even rising above or going beyond them? The first step is to identify the enemy to be conquered. An unseen enemy is often victorious over you. You cannot triumph over anything you do not acknowledge.

I had to call the enemy out by name. Despair was despair. I could not keep calling it a bad day or a long night. Fear was fear. Guilt was guilt—not me trying to figure out what I should have or could have done. Anger was anger. Unforgiveness was unforgiveness—not simply my remembering what happened. The best way to win a fight is to attack from behind. A powerful blow to the back of someone's head who is unsuspecting will knock him out or at the very least bring him down to his knees.

Similar things may happen to many burn survivors emotionally. You can be fine, progressing well, and all of a sudden something unexpected happens, and you are not emotionally prepared: Your breathing becomes complicated, and you have to be put back on the ventilator. You contract a staph infection, and now you're critically ill. Your kidneys stop functioning properly, and now you have dialysis to deal with. Doctors thought they would be able to save your foot, but gangrene has set in and now they have to amputate.

The scenarios can be endless. So how do you rise above those type of circumstances? The same way the clobbered person does. You regain control, turn around, face your assailant, and attack. Regaining control is simply accepting what is going on—not wishing it weren't like this or calling reality something else. It is what it is. Turning around is determining you are going to try to help yourself as much as possible and then doing everything you can do to make the situation better. Facing your assailant is looking your circumstance in the eye and not fearing it. Finally, it is time to attack, applying peace, patience, and endurance every step of the way.

The second crucial step in achieving triumph is to deal with, rather than bury, problems. Buried problems unearth themselves sooner or later and make a wreck of the foundation you are working to build. When I homeschooled my children before the fire, I had a ritual I would do at the start of each year. I would begin with a prayer for the year to be blessed.

I would remind my boys, "Momma was blessed to teach this year, but we don't know what next year may hold. Therefore, we are going to be thankful for this year and give it our best."

I wanted to put them and myself on guard, just in case something happened. Dad could lose his job, and then we couldn't afford it. I could get sick and not be able to do it. Any number of things could happen.

Finally, something did happen. Fire came and destroyed our home, leaving our family devastated. My friend Lori had finished homeschooling my class for me that year. The next school year, it was my husband's and my decision to modify our schooling. As many times as I gave that speech, I wasn't prepared to let go of the boys. We compromised and chose the video homeschool program. That way, I was not responsible for teaching, just administering tests and paperwork.

The year was awful. I was disconnected emotionally, still in pain physically, and the boy's homeschool experience turned sour as a result. The problem was I was neither ready nor able to do homeschooling. Instead of dealing with it, I buried the truth and tried to go on anyway. Tragic mistake.

My freshman year in high school, I was on the varsity girls' basketball team. I was a decent player, but I wasn't used to organized sports. I had a run-in with the coach right off. I wanted to shoot from one spot on the court only. He couldn't understand why I wouldn't take shots from other places. The skill was obviously there, and my form was perfect. Still, I refused to shoot unless I was dead center in front of the free throw line. From there, I would swish the net every time. I could shoot that shot blind.

The ironic thing about it was that is exactly what I was doing: shooting blind. I couldn't see that net for anything. I couldn't see the chalkboard at school or anything more than a few yards away. I was nearsighted, and I knew it. I had been since I could remember. How that got past my mother, I don't know. It was a buried problem that I refused to deal with. I could have asked my mother to get my eyes checked, but there was another problem. I didn't want to wear glasses. I didn't like the solution.

Many times we don't deal with issues because we don't care for the solution. My coach figured out what was going on within the first few practices. He bought me my first pair of glasses, Jordache, and I became a force to reckon with on the court. The same will be true for you when you take the time to do what you know you have to do.

The third step in achieving victory in your present reality is to use every resource available to you. It is amazing how many resources, external and internal, are at our disposal. There was nothing more encouraging for me than to have a burn survivor say to me, "You can make it." He was a testimony of triumph standing before me, someone I could focus on when I was most discouraged. Here was an external resource that roared, "I made it, and you can too."

The nurses, therapists, and doctors are also excellent external resources. They are voices of experience and compassion with triumph in mind themselves. Expanding the list of external resources are family, friends, and spiritual overseers, each with a personal stake in your well-being. Your victory is their victory as well. Your internal composition should be employed in the fight also. Even the not-so-flattering side is useful.

I redefined stubborn. It was a curse to me in my childhood days. I got into more trouble because I would not change courses for anything or anyone. I was adamant about my beliefs. But this trait is also the reason I have the use of my hands today.

During a clinic visit for a post-surgery checkup, my surgeon, Dr. Parks, was examining my hands, turning them palm up and then palm down, admiring his own work it seemed. Then he made a casual comment.

"They turned out really nice, Tina. Just think, I was going to amputate them. But when I saw your stubbornness while you were in a coma, I knew you would do what it would take to make use of them again. So here we are."

He smiled.

I was appalled.

My husband had not told me that the doctors considered amputating my hands. Thank God for my stubbornness! That's what saved my hands.

We have many internal resources to employ; faith, patience, love, and hope are just a few. Putting them to use and giving them a task can help you triumph.

If there is one thing in this world that you do have control over, it is your joy, and why let a situation or any circumstance rob you of that? Of course, there will be darkness at times, but there is ALWAYS the light at the end of the tunnel. You can turn any tragedy into a triumph. You choose.
—**Chandra Berns**, burn survivor, "Three for Hope"

The final step—and the most difficult step—is to fight until you win. Endure. Hang in there, and never give up. One of the most fascinating stories in the Bible to me is that of Jacob wrestling with the angel. The scriptures say that they wrestled until daybreak. The angel told Jacob to let him go. Jacob responded with a powerful statement: "I will not let you go until you bless me" ().

I integrated Jacob's statement into my mindset while I was on the burn unit. I was determined not to let go until I had won, until I was triumphant. I wrestled until fear, anger, unforgiveness, and pain were subject to me. I fought until I gleaned every bit of wisdom I could get from those foes and then began to build upon that. Tenacity is a good and true friend to embrace during a traumatic experience.

When I was a sophomore in college, I moved from the dormitory to an apartment with June above a pizza parlor. I had a good friend named Deirdra with whom I studied often in the apartment. We discovered that the pizza restaurant had a policy that would work in our favor: The owner would throw away any pizza order that wasn't picked up within an hour.

The idea formed in both our heads at the same time. We wondered if he would just give us the pizza instead of throwing it away. It made sense to us.

To test our theory, we had to suffer an inconvenience. We had to spend time at the restaurant and wait on the order that was not picked up. It would involve time and the chance that it might not happen. But Deirdra and I had something in common: we were both tenacious. When we decided we were going to do something, that is what we did.

My college years were one of the poorest times in my life. A free meal in the form of pizza was equivalent to gold. So we packed our book bags, took a seat, and studied as we waited for the prize. Many college students studied there, but usually they were studying over the pizza they bought.

The first day, we refused to buy a pizza, or couldn't buy one, so we just sat there waiting for our reward. We would time the orders when they came in so that in sixty minutes flat, we could start begging. Most people picked up their pizza, but we refused to give up.

Three hours later, our tenacity paid off. The owner was glad to give us the pizza, though a little shocked to see us sit there so long for that purpose. I told him I lived above him, and he even went a step further. He began to set the pizzas aside during the day for us to pick up.

Here's the point: Giving up will rob you of triumph every time. Not trying will keep you from the road all together. Even when it's tough, unfair, or inconvenient, hang in there. The reward is at the end, and your life may depend on it.

Triumph is all about winning and overcoming the odds. The measurement of triumph is personal. It varies like the flowers all over the earth. It is a step-by-step achievement. My first triumph was to live. That was followed by waking up from a coma. Then it was being able to endure the scrubs. Eventually, my victory was being able to sit up. I was grateful for every milestone achieved. The more I accomplished, the more I went for.

I had an athlete's mentality: win. Winning was engrained in me. I had trained as an athlete most of my life. Still, I needed to set reasonable goals; otherwise, I may have been overtaken with discouragement.

Justina Page with NASA astronauts training on burn unit

Prayer

Heavenly Father, I come to you in the name of Jesus.
Thank You! You have carried me and helped me through so much.
Truly, you have made all things work together for my good.
I admit I could not see these days a few months ago.
I never thought I would have my independence and joy back.
But, you are faithful, and I am ever so grateful.
Please continue to bring me to the place you would have me to be.
Guide me in helping others achieve the triumph they so desire.
I want everyone to have thevictory I feel right now.
In Jesus' name,
Amen.

Chapter 20

THE REAL YOU UNVEILED

Life is wonderful, not because trials have never come my way nor because I believe they will never surface again. Rather, life is perfect simply because I have it.

I have now shed the layers of pain, anger, unforgiveness, fear, and guilt. Beneath that skin is a more stable, wise, and thankful person. My faith is intact and as strong as ever. Life is wonderful, not because trials have never come my way nor because I believe they will never surface again. Rather, life is perfect simply because I have it. I feel better prepared for it. I am so thankful to be among the living. I have learned to cherish everyone and everything I have. I take nothing and no one for granted. I am learning to make the most of the day that is at hand.

So many people are miserable because of tomorrow, a day they may or may not see. Every precious person and moment is a gift. I realize that no one owes me anything. It's a liberating way to live because my expectations for others are low, making whatever they do a big deal.

Who we really are is normally buried under visible things, such as clothes, friends, status, and accomplishments. A burn trauma has a way of stripping you bare, showing you for the person you really are. I found myself lying in a hospital bed, owning nothing but my integrity. After the fire destroyed my home and ravished my body, who was I then? I was known to be the lady who loved purple, an enviable homemaker, and a confidant. But when I owned nothing, and purple didn't matter, when I didn't have the ability to take care of my household, and couldn't shoulder a burden for the life of me, who was I then?

Despair said I was nothing. I had to reach deep to clothe myself. I knew I was a fighter, but I never had to fight at this level before. I was a woman of faith; the horror of the devastation brought that to the surface. I loved my kids. I had run through and not away from fire to save them. I loved and trusted my husband. He was a source of consolation daily. I loved Jesus. I trusted him to bring me through. I was blessed. The evidence was everywhere.

My pastor once taught us that our actions are who we want to be, but our reaction is who we really are, a powerful revelation that keeps me grounded and clothed with humility. I might smile and speak ever so softly, but if my reactions are consistently frowns and yells, the real me is not the peaceful soul I present but a distraught soul I'm hiding.

My reaction to our fire was enlightening. I became acutely aware of what necessity was and what luxury was. Tragedy had sifted folly to a fine powder, and suffering had blown it away. When I did entertain foolishness, it was by choice and not ignorance. It's amazing how trauma can sharpen your spiritual senses.

Amos House of Faith Proclamation Day award from Mayor Bill White

The fear of the Lord is the instruction of wisdom; and before honour is humility (Prov. 15:33).
—**Demetria Austin**, friend

One of our longest-standing activities as children was dancing school. Dancing school began at the age of three and lasted until you graduated from high school. It was a time-consuming extracurricular activity. We didn't have much choice but to attend.

The Smith Sisters Dance Studio was run by two sisters, one of which lived on our block and was good friends with my grandmother. My aunts had gone to dancing school. My siblings and cousins went to dancing school. My nieces and nephews go to dancing school. We participated in everything: ballet, tap, jazz, acrobat, toe, baton, and drill team.

When I was in seventh grade, I began to notice a trend. The better you were, the harder the teachers pushed. Dancing school was just a pastime for me. I wasn't interested in performing in the Nutcracker. In the eighth grade, I began an experiment. I purposely displayed only part of my talent. That way, when the push came from my instructors, I was still at a comfortable level. No one picked up on what I was doing because the seventy-five percent I was giving was decent. They just figured I was not as talented as my older sister.

Kelly had a vested interest in being pushed. She was interested in a career on the stage. As I reached high school and my athletic and scholastic activities increased, I eventually grew sick of dancing school. It became a nuisance as my interest dwindled. Still, I hung in there till my senior year.

Every year we would have a dance recital at the municipal hall. The custom was for senior year students to be showcased, center stage, in the routine of their choice. I chose jazz. My jazz class was performing the finale that year to Prince's hit "Let's Go Crazy." It was the last performance I was ever going to do. I was elated.

As I assumed my position front and center, before the lights came on, I had a fleeting thought: *Why don't I show them what I can really do and who I really am?* The lights came on, and something came over me. My body language, my attitude, and whole demeanor were possessed by this professional dancer no one knew existed. Kicks, tucks, and leaps were coming from nowhere. I didn't even know that level of talent was in me. The instructors sitting below the stage were on their feet. I glimpsed my sister on the side of the stage with an enormous grin on her face. The audience was wild.

After the recital, my dance instructor approached me and asked, "Why did you hold back on us?"

I answered as honestly as I could: "Because I didn't want the pressure of showing you the real me."

The statement from years ago sounds a lot like the sentiments of many burn survivors today. It is pressure trying to show the real you to a world that doesn't readily accept you for who you are or what you can do. Sometimes you don't even get the chance.

I look back over my dancing school days and wish I could correct my thinking. My craftiness in holding back didn't take anything from them; it only hurt me. As an adult, I can see now that if I had allowed myself to be pushed, it would not have only improved my dancing skills but my athletic and life skills as well. Life can be a demanding instructor. When you learn one lesson, another lesson is right on your heels. This is good for us. It drives us to be the best we can be.

Unveiling the real you is a process in which the superficial covering hiding the true treasure within you is lifted away. The real you, the soul, is ushered to the forefront, mainly because the places for you to hide have been drastically limited. We are seldom whom we appear to be anyway. We can hide our true identity behind a mirage of things, such as money, fame, popularity, and works. But when those things are temporarily shut down, we are inclined to search for the person and purpose God has established for us to embody.

David said it most eloquently in the book of Psalms: "We are fearfully and wonderfully made" (). Each and every one of us was created with so much love and purpose in mind. Our makeup is so unique to us that I could never be you, and you could never be me. It is amazing how that a single fingerprint can distinguish me from several other billion people in the world.

Tragedy is not the only way to draw out the person you really are. Neither is the purpose of tragedy to discover who you are. Tragedy's purpose is found in the wisdom we draw from our experience. We can, however, learn from any situation.

Opportunity is also a strong avenue for self-discovery. When I was fourteen years old, I began working a summer job at the Youth Summer Sports Program in Kansas City, Missouri. I was given the ten-year-old girls' group to lead. My responsibilities included chaperoning them to their various activities for the day, assisting those who were having a hard time, and offering minor counseling. I was drenched in excitement about getting my first job, joyful in expectation of the checks that would follow. Those paydays would allow me to shop, what I loved to do most.

Still, I was a little apprehensive. I took the responsibility of leadership seriously. I had attended the same program as a child every summer. The memory of the leaders I had when I was ten is still clear today: the way they primped themselves when they thought none of us were paying attention; how they showed disapproval at our appearance; and their obvious disinterest in us as people. We were just a job for them.

How I had wanted to connect with those pretty girls and ask so many questions about life, but they did not open the door for that opportunity. I was determined not to be like them. On my first day as group leader, I made every girl in my group fill out a questionnaire about herself.

One of the girls asked me in a subdued voice, "Is this something new they are starting? We never had to do this before."

I explained to her that I wanted to do it so that I could get to know them all better. A ripple of excitement spread through the group. That small outreach was the start of a bond that lasted for years and made a significant impact in their lives. I won leader of the year that summer, and at the girls' request, I followed them as leader for the next two years I worked there.

The opportunity to work at the summer youth program was the beginning of self-discovery for me. I learned that compassion was a part of my fabric. I learned how much I loved working with children and even discovered how closely I analyze others' behavior. King Solomon said in the book of Proverbs that a man's gift will make room for him (). In many cases, opportunity is the cover waiting to be drawn in order for the person we are, the story of our lives, to be unveiled.

I was on my high school cheerleading squad for four years: freshman, sophomore, and two years on the varsity squad. I was definitely not interested in wearing miniskirts, waving pom-poms, and freezing during football season. My true love was sports, especially basketball. I was a six-foot-tall pole. I only joined the cheerleading team because a classmate mockingly said I couldn't make the team. She was deceived and didn't know me well. All she saw was my surface abilities, the ones I chose to reveal.

Everyone knew I was a tomboy and that I could hold my own running and playing ball with the boys. What this one classmate didn't know was that I had been in dancing school since age three, in a major drill team, and was on a tumbling team. I never showed that side of my life to my classmates. I loved to be underestimated. I was actually going to the tryouts to support my friend Vickie who wanted to be on the freshman squad. I had helped her with her cheer and gave her some pointers on how to make herself stand out. Out of fifty or more girls, only eight would be chosen.

As we walked into the gym, one of the girls looked our way and began to laugh. Big mistake. I walked right up to her.

"Are you laughing at me?" I asked in an offended tone.

She looked sheepishly toward the floor and then covered her mouth.

"It's just that it is really funny to think of you as a cheerleader, T. Are you seriously going to try out? You'll never make it."

I was incensed. I wanted to shout at her and tell her about the million abilities I had, but I decided instead to do something more powerful. Forget talking; I would show her. I turned from her and never said another word.

As I approached the sign-up table, the look of unbelief on every face tripled my determination. Now I had to become a cheerleader. Vickie raced behind me, taking two steps for every step I made in order to match my long strides.

She whispered in a frightened voice, "What are you doing?"

I ignored her. I was totally silent until the judges called me forward to give my name and do my cheer. I announced in a confident voice that my name was Justina Robinson, and then I turned fierce eyes toward the mocker and said, "And I will be your next freshman squad captain."

The silence was so thick you could feel it. I began with a round off and a quick back flip series, landing perfectly. I immediately did three of the five jumps they had asked to see, even though we were only required to do one as freshmen. I choreographed my routine on the spot.

When I finished, the whole gym and judging table were on their feet, clapping and yelling approval.

"I had no idea you could do that!" Vickie said in disbelief.

"I had no reason to show you," I responded.

I had no reason to show you. Now that I think about it, that was an interesting statement if I do say so myself. Sometimes all you need is a reason to show everyone that you can do it, that you can make it.

At that time, I finally had a reason to show them. When I found myself on the burn unit with the odds against me—chaos infiltrating my peace and hope playing hide and seek—I had no other choice but to show the world what I could do. Life's unwelcomed tragedies have a way of pushing the real you forward.

Most people can only see what we choose to show them. It was important for me to show others *and* myself what I could do.

> *I was burned on over seventy percent of my body in a motorcycle explosion at the age of fourteen, which resulted in a three-week-long coma, life support, and eight months of hospitalization. After discharge from the hospital, I attempted to hide away from the world in a self-imposed isolation for two years in my parents' home. We are each faced with choices every day, and I finally made the conscious choice to **"unveil the real me"** as I began looking at myself as a burn survivor. Life now has meaning, purpose, and fulfillment as I reconnected to my higher power and acknowledged my humble, yet glorious position as a child of God.*
> —**Dennis Gardin**, executive director, Georgia Burn Foundation

When I left the hospital, my friends, family, and church family made me feel so comfortable that I was almost not conscious of my burns. Everybody treated me as he always had. Thus, when I was out in public and someone began staring at me, it took a few minutes for it to register that he was staring at my burns.

I am no longer trapped by the scars on my body. I have come full circle. I am as active as ever. I still work with kids, implement programs, fellowship with my church family, enjoy my kids, and date my husband. I do what I feel God would have me to do. I choose not to let others or society have a say in that.

It all comes down to a decision—the choice we make to live our lives to the fullest or cave in under the pressure. I don't mean to make light of the pressure. It is real. There are a million valid excuses for burn survivors who have experienced heartbreak and disappointment to give up and never communicate with society again.

But not one of those excuses can negate the reality of the purpose for you being here. The mere fact that you are living is a testament to your value on the earth. The way you perceive yourself is the foundation upon which you will set your ambitions. If you see yourself as nothing, you will seek nothing. You are a burn survivor, not a burn victim. A burn victim is one who is harmed, lost, and destroyed. Burn survivors stand on top of their tragedy and build their lives from there.

Justina receiving HFD Hometown Hero Award

Prayer

Heavenly Father, I come to you in the name of Jesus.
I don't want to be anyone else but who you made me to be.
Help me to discover who I am and be content with that.
I have learned so many things during this tragedy—
some good and some bad.
Help me to improve in the areas that are harmful to me and others.
I want to deal in reality and not try to be my neighbor.
I know that the plans that you have for me are good and not evil.
You have said the plans you have are thoughts of peace
and good that will bring me to an expected end.
I am not afraid of who I am, and I am not afraid
to show the world what you have designed.
Thank you for your strength.
In Jesus' name,
Amen.

Chapter 21

SUNSHINE RETURNS

He hath made every thing beautiful in his time–Ecclesiastes 3:11

I could not sleep for the life of me. I would close my eyes, take slow, deep breaths, and try to relax, but a smile kept invading my face. My eyes would fly open, and giggles would spill from my throat. I would flip flop from my right side to my left side and back again. I would press my face into the pillow, but it was no use. I was way too excited.

I looked at the clock. Goodness, it was only two o'clock in the morning. A tall, masculine frame approached the door to my hospital room.

"Having problems falling asleep?" a hint of smile was in his voice. He was a compassionate and caring man and one of my favorite nighttime nurses.

"Yes," I said, exasperated with myself.

"Don't feel bad," he said as he stepped a little further in the doorway. "Many of the patients are like that the night before they go home. Sometimes talking about it helps."

I was so glad he understood.

"Turn the light on and take a seat," I said as I sat up a little, and he adjusted the pillows for my back. The opportunity to talk was exactly what I needed.

He sat in the chair with his fingers intertwined, crossing his right foot over his left knee. He assumed a relaxed position and smiled. It was obvious he had done this a thousand times before. He initiated the conversation.

"So, tell me about your family. They seem really nice."

That was my topic of choice anyway—especially that night as I would be reunited with them in the morning. We would be a family again, living in our own home. I went into a long, drawn-out discourse about the characteristics of each child. The time away from them gave me time to ponder their individual personalities, and it sharpened my ability to analyze them.

I was very detailed, even with Amos. It was still painful to talk about Amos, but I refused to leave him out of the family description. He was and is my son. I talked about my hero, my husband, which drew out occasional groans of agreement from the nurse. He would leave periodically to check on his other patients, but he always returned, patiently letting me pour out my memories of the past and my hopes for the future.

In the middle of one of my many discourses, I looked out the window. The sun was coming up. I smiled and told him, "It's time for me to pack." Sunshine had returned again.

There's a major highway in Houston called Interstate 610. It is the inner loop, a large circle that goes around the entire city. One time a friend who was coming to visit me from Tulsa needed directions to get to my house. The exit she needed was on 610. She called me about fifteen minutes after I had given her the directions and said she had missed her exit and had been traveling on 610 for a long time. I told her to not worry about it. Then I explained to her why: The 610 highway is nothing more than a circle. If you keep traveling on it, you will get to the exit you need.

I feel the same way about those who are experiencing a burn trauma. The tragedy is a big loop with many exits. If you miss your exit, your chance to overcome the obstacle facing you, don't worry. Keep traveling. The exit you need will appear again.

Dealing with the fire and all of the circumstances that transpired as a result was heavy. There were many hours of pain and suffering involved. There were equal amounts of self- discovery and growth. There were times when I felt all was lost and I wasn't going to make it another day. There were times I could see myself climbing Mount Everest.

At the end of it all, I won. Not because I was so strong or good, but because God was good. He gave me the gift of time. Time was a good friend to me. In time, I was restored, body, mind, and soul. God made all things beautiful for me in his time.

Sunshine returned when my faith was revitalized. It happened the moment I stepped back on God's track and got off of mine, the point when I realized that the same God who was holding me before the fire held me through the fire and would continue to hold me as long as my faith and trust were in him.

Page boys 2009

Chapter 22

OUR SONS

The road has not always been easy.

When my husband asked me to be the mother of his children, I had no idea how profound that request was. I was flattered to think that he not only saw me as a desirable life partner, but also as a guide for his home and as a nurturer to his family. Twenty–eight years, six sons, and two grandchildren later, I have come to cherish the request and the subsequent fulfilled calling. James and I have been a team of one. We are focused on one purpose for our family: to fulfill God's will in our lives. We are driven by one force: Jesus.

The road has not always been easy. There have been many tumultuous times. But the hardships have been obscured by the wonderful experiences and joys that come with having six, vibrant boys in your charge. There are many priceless moments of time etched in my memory that I would not trade for the world. We are a cozy group. Everyone in his respective place, enjoying God's blessings and each other.

The house fire shook everything up for all of us and especially for our children. The boys were forced to mature at an incredibly fast pace. Before they even reached their teenage years, they had to tackle and process serious issues, such as death, loss, and pain—issues that many adults strive a lifetime to understand or overcome. By the grace of God, they have travelled that challenging terrain called tragedy and are all the better for it.

I lose everything that is mine.
—Jonathon Page

Page Jr. Family 2012

Grandson
Amos J. Page

Grandughter
Jyelle R. Page

Before the fire, Jonathon was a nine-year-old homeschooler who was shielded from many of the injustices of this world. He was a natural leader and competitive by nature. He took the role of big brother to another level. His nine-year-old determination to see to the fun and safety of his younger brothers was admirable. Jonathon is also honest to a fault. Half-truths never worked for him.

I remember a library activity that our homeschool group did where the children were to take turns standing in front of the group and make up a short story. Jonathon could not grasp the concept. In his seven-year-old mind, making up stories was the same as lying, and he wasn't having it. Things were true, or they were false. Out of sheer frustration, I agreed to his request to let him share what he called "a real story." Jonathon proceeded to quote an entire book that I had read to him the previous day, verbatim. Everyone was astonished.

That activity shed quite a bit of light on his character and gifts. It also taught me two very important things about him. First, whatever I said was truth. So, when I tucked him in bed and told him to sleep tight and that God was watching over him, then he believed God was responsible for what happened that night. Secondly, Jonathon would stick to that truth no matter what anyone else did. There are no gray areas with him. Things are either right or wrong. The unfortunate loss of his baby brother shredded that precious trust and challenged his own beliefs.

After several twist and turns, he has been realigned with his faith and is in full pursuit of God's will for his life. He is a striking, twenty-five-year-old bachelor—if I do say so myself—working two jobs and crafting a master plan for his own business. Look out, world. There is a serious entrepreneur in the making.

> *I am a coward. Remember the fire? I only saved myself.*
> **—Joseph Page**

There is a comical moment in the midst of the house fire that our family looks back on with amusement. All of us lost every single possession we had—except Joseph. Joseph escaped with his money, his bills and coins. He had always been a stickler about managing his finances and possessions from a very young age. On the rare occasions when we would buy each of the boys a package of mixed candies, the other boys would tear into their bags without thought, but not Joseph. He would separate the pieces in groups and make his candy last for days.

Joseph is the son who puts thought and reflection into anything he does, a true mark of maturity. He has never been afraid to be himself. The bravery displayed by his father and elder brother in attempting to rescue the family during the fire caused him to question his own self-worth. Fortunately, he has come to terms with what defines a courageous man.

Joseph recently graduated from the University of Houston and works at Centerpoint Energy. He is twenty-four, teaches Sunday school, and holds a "Young Man You Can" meeting with youth boys. He is also strikingly handsome, but unfortunately not available. He is happily married to Naomi, his new queen, and they have blessed us with two wonderful grandchildren, Amos and Jyelle Page. He is fierce in his devotion to God and family. There is nothing cowardly about this young man.

They are nice when you are around, but when
you leave, they talk about you and tease me.
—Caleb Page

When the fire occurred, Caleb was in first grade, a time when one is just learning to branch out in the world alone. He has always been the Momma's boy, safe and secure playing in Momma's presence. He was in no way prepared for the trauma to come. My husband and I had always provided him unconditional love and acceptance. The world challenged his assurance of belonging after the fire.

Caleb endured the most teasing, which caused him to search for acceptance at any cost. Time, love, and prayer has brought him to a place of stability. He is a peculiar child that pipes to his own tune. Wherever life takes him, I know that the end destiny will be greatness.

Caleb's career goal is to own his own hotel. I thought it was an odd career choice, but when I mentioned it to his grandmother during a phone conversation, she informed me that my deceased uncle once owned his own hotel in Denver, Colorado. So it seems that this interest runs in the blood. Who knew? Caleb is twenty-two and also strikingly handsome. Taller than all of his brothers, at 6'6", he is equally towering in his compassion for others.

Daniel has grown into a very handsome young man. He enjoys soccer, movies, and especially music. His gift for music was likely handed down to him from his paternal line, all of whom are very accomplished singers and musicians. He will not sing for you by request, but we often catch him singing when he is alone. He has a melodious voice just like his father.

Daniel still has a hankering for the silverware. We thought we would outsmart him and buy a safe for our metal silverware and give him plastic utensils. Our success was short lived. We noticed the forks and spoons slowly dwindling away. I soon found out that Daniel had somehow managed to break open the back of the safe and get the silverware anyway. They say if you can't beat 'em, then join 'em. Now we ask Daniel if we can borrow a fork for dinner.

Benjamin is still everyone's boy. The charm that boy has is a direct gift from God. Of course, *man*, not boy, is what you think of when you see Benjamin. My baby is 6'4" and weighs nearly three hundred pounds. He is intimidating at first sight, but so approachable and lovable when you reach out to him. Benjamin has always enjoyed sports and basketball most of all. He is a force to reckon with on the court.

I was picking Ben and Dan up from school one day when I was approached by Ben's teacher and all of the aids. It was the Friday of the first week of school, and I could not fathom what Ben could have done to draw all of the staff to my car. I tried to wave and take off quickly, but I was flagged down. In my mind, I was thinking, *This news must be really bad.* The teacher gestured for me to roll down the window and proceeded to tell me that the football coaches had been observing Ben all week. They wanted to know how much he understood about football and if I thought he could join the team. I politely told them no and laughed all the way home. His size and build has scouts looking at him till this day.

As a mother, your first concern is the well-being and prosperity of your children. First and foremost of all concerns is their eternal safety. All of my children have accepted Christ as their Lord and Savior. Despite all the trying and dark times, God has managed to draw each one to him. That assurance, in and of itself, has given me my greatest joy. I know my boys will prosper, even as their souls prosper. God has made me a joyful mother of children. I wouldn't trade my crew for all the tea in China.

Prayer

Lord, we are so thankful for all of your many blessings.
We are thankful for the strength you have given us to
endure this journey and the wisdom we have gained.
We have lived Romans 8:28 and are assured it will not fail:
"And we know that all things work together for good to them
that love God and are the called according to his purpose."
We trust you.
In Jesus' name,
Amen.

AFTERWORD

Trapped inside of you is a vision that can change the world. Unleash it.
—Justina Page

It was a rare moment. I was alone. My mind was wrestling with my dissatisfaction. Why do the caretakers of burn survivors not have a place near the hospital to stay while they look after their critically injured loved ones? Who is looking after their many needs? What about the kids who have faced life-altering injuries or who have lost someone? Who is helping them deal with their problems?

I felt someone needed to do something. Then I felt the tap on my shoulder. The question that birthed my new found purpose was resounding in my mind: *What are you doing?*

I was doing what everyone else was doing, namely, complaining. I decided then and there that Amos's death would not be in vain. I would use this atrocious event as a stepping stone and build a house of hope for those who had the same unfortunate experience we had. In Amos's memory, I founded The Amos House of Faith, a nonprofit organization that provides support for children and families affected by burn trauma.

That decision catapulted me into the burn community, where I discovered many uses for my various talents. I had always been a leader, a visionary, and a nurturer. That community needed those gifts in abundance.

I was determined to do something. I wanted to help. I felt prompted to serve others and to display hope. This was not a disposition foreign to me, but I had never had the platform or opportunity to serve at this level. I believe the greater the experience, the greater the call to serve after you walk through it. I was sure my experience would benefit someone. God had made all things to work together for good—even this wretched fire.

Sometimes I rode buses and borrowed cars to fulfill the vision within. I would schedule one meeting this week, maybe two the next, striving for the goals that were set before me. I slowly and consistently expanded my networking base, establishing a foundation to offer the much-needed services for the burn community in my area. I joined various organizations and volunteered with others.

Eventually, I rose to positions of leadership in all of them. I could hear the words of my pastor's wife, which she expressed on several occasions, echoing in my ear, "You are a natural-born leader." The gift of leadership was fine-tuned by the tragedy I suffered. I pleaded my cause before audiences of one, groups of affluence, and men of wealth, striving to establish The Amos House of Faith, a nonprofit organization named in memory of my son and intended to bless families affected by burn trauma in the greater Houston metropolitan area. The tenacity and faith it took to build the organization is astonishing. We have since been sprinkled with honors and accolades, but the humble beginnings I will never forget.

It was February of 2006. I was volunteering at the hospital, running a booth for the SOAR program during Burn Awareness Month. As providence would have it, the booth next to me belonged to the Houston Fire Department Community Outreach Program.

I was in full presenting mode when a slightly built firefighter with kind eyes and a coal-black, well-groomed, full mustache stretched his hand toward me and introduced himself.

"Hello, there. My name is Captain Bennett. I am the head of HFD Community Outreach." His manner bespoke kindness.

I reached my partially amputated hand toward him, secretly measuring his response, and said, "Justina, I volunteer on the burn unit here. I'm here sharing information about the SOAR program we recently started. SOAR stands for Survivors Offering Assistance and Recovery to burn survivors. It is a program established by the Phoenix Society for Burn Survivors to provide peer support—"

He cut me off. I was well into my practiced spiel about SOAR and hadn't realized that he had taken a step closer to me and was looking me directly in the eyes. He spoke with authority, "What is it that you want to do? I see vision all in your eyes."

I was taken aback. It was as if he had been given a front-row seat in my heart, with a view of a dream that I had not revealed to anyone. I had already written my idea off as impossible—at least for me to accomplish in the real world. I lifted my left eyebrow and pursed my lip. My answer was hesitant, "Do you really want to know?"

He folded his arms in front of him, taking on a military stance. A grin slowly spread across his face. "Of course I do."

I trusted him—something I personally don't do easily and definitely not with a first-time acquaintance. But, I really had an innate sense to trust him. I was strongly prompted in my heart to share my ideas with him. My dream was precious, and unlike the make-believe of my childhood, I sincerely hoped it could come true. My vision was driven by the memory of my beloved twin son Amos. I would not tolerate it being meddled with or treated irreverently. I would rather hold the dream safe and protected in my heart.

"I want to build a nonprofit in memory of the son I lost in a fire in 1999. I want to assist children and families through their burn-trauma journey. I want to provide some of the services for burn survivors and their caregivers that are so desperately needed in the burn community here in Houston. I want to inspire them and offer hope."

He was silent for a while. Then he reached in his pocket, pulled out a business card, and handed it to me.

"Let's do it. I'll help you. It can be done," he said in a confident voice as he instructed me to call him the next day.

We made small talk for the duration of the event, further introducing ourselves. Hope blossomed in my heart that day. A seed of faith had been planted.

For the first time, I actually believed that the vision I had would make its way out of dreamland and rest safely on the shores of reality.

Captain Bennett made good on his promise. Our first meeting was the launching pad for The Amos House of Faith.

From the ashes of my tragedy, a new hope has arisen.

My hope is to provide support groups tailor-made for children who have been affected by burn trauma. That includes children who have been burned or who have lost someone due to a burn injury. Their siblings are included as well. I want to provide a home away from home for the caregivers of seriously burned patients so that they may be close to their loved ones.

When a patient is life-flighted in to the hospital, he is generally coming from a nearby city, close enough to home to get the help he needs quickly, but far enough away to be a financial burden and stress in his prolonged hospital stay. Many caregivers cannot afford the costly parking and food that an extended visit to the hospital requires. Many of them sleep in waiting rooms, refusing to leave their loved one during that critical period. I plan to provide a facility that will accommodate them and offer a place of support and encouragement.

I know firsthand how traumatic a burn injury can be and the immeasurable benefit of post-burn support. I have dedicated myself to those going through this horrific experience. It is my way of giving back to the community that helped me through my long and arduous recovery. I know that tragedies like mine can happen to anyone. When they do, the families involved will need all of the love and support possible to sustain their hope.

The nonprofit organization named in honor of my son—The Amos House of Faith—provides post-burn support for children and families affected by burn trauma. Every time a child, burn victim, or caregiver is helped, I am comforted that Amos's death had a purpose. It is a very satisfying and soothing recompense, like medicine. Many burn survivors have found their purpose is established within the burn community.

Before the fire, I had never met anyone who was burned. I was oblivious to the plight of a burn patient. You could not have told me in the 1980s that my entire life would be centered around finding resources for families and helping them navigate through burn-trauma situations. My mind was focused on corporate America. I had already tasted the fruit of corporate life by working at ATT Technologies as a summer intern before I went to college. I envisioned myself the CEO of a Fortune 500 company; kids and a husband were nowhere in the picture. But it is better to go where purpose leads. I am proud and perfectly content that my initial vision was disrupted. I am fulfilled in the role of godly wife and mother, as He has called me to be. All other purposes flow from that calling.

All journeys lead somewhere—even the difficult ones. Difficult journeys can often have a satisfying end, especially when there is an unseen, guiding hand, directing a purpose all the while. So it was with our family. In the middle of the journey, there was pain, fear, guilt, and anger. We faced many difficult situations that have altered our lives forever. We began with faith, and we ended with stronger faith. We started as a close-knit unit and ended as a closer-knit family.

Amos lives on in each of our hearts. He will never be forgotten. The vision we have is to use our experience and knowledge to assist others through the difficult journey of burn-trauma recovery. In the near future, we hope to open The Amos House of Faith Family Room. This facility will house the caretakers of severely burned patients and provide some of their daily needs, such as food and parking. I continue to advocate for a fire-safe America through the various organizations I work for.

We have overcome it all. But we didn't do it alone. God was with us, and many generous souls helped along the way. We take nothing for granted and are thankful for everything we have.

ABC Club Houston Field Trip

*ABC Club Houston
HFD Apparatus Visit*

*Manny Gonzalez ABC Club
Houston volunteer*

ABC Club Houston

*ABC Club Houston Fire Museum
Field Trip*

*ABC Club Houston
Mother's Day Project*

I HAVE A SON IN GLORY

I have a son in glory,
Beholding our Lord's face.
Surrounded by the angels,
In a predestinated place.
Separated from earthly loved ones,
Who miss him day by day,
Yet comforted in knowing
We'll meet again one day.
—Justina Page

PRAYER INDEX

ABOUT THE AUTHOR

Justina Page's life was changed forever in the early morning hours of March 7, 1999. That is when fire swept through her Houston home, killing her twenty-two-month-old son Amos and severely injuring his twin brother, Benjamin. She was left with third-degree burns over 55 percent of her body.

From the ashes of this tragedy, a new hope has risen.

Justina has since dedicated herself to helping families affected by burn trauma. She is the founder and executive director of The Amos House of Faith, a nonprofit organization established to provide post-burn support to children and families affected by burn trauma.

Justina's work within the burn community has been recognized by various organizations. Those accolades include the following honors: 2008 Memorial Hermann Hospital Volunteer of the Year; Houston Fire Department Neighborhood Hero Award; Houston Texas's Halliburton Hometown Hero Award; Shriner's Hospital for Children in Galveston 2008 Volunteer Group of the Year Award; and the Mayor Bill White Amos House of Faith Proclamation Day.

Being a burn survivor herself, as well as the mother of burn survivors, she has experienced all the stages of trauma a burn patient faces and is specifically qualified to deal with these problems. Through the Phoenix Society for Burn Survivors, she has been trained as a SOAR (Survivors Offering Assistance and Recovery) trainer, coordinator, and peer supporter. This, coupled with her work at the John S. Dunn Sr. Burn Center at Memorial Hermann Hospital, Shriners Hospital in Galveston, and the Phoenix Society, gives her a deep understanding of how to teach, help, and inspire others.

Justina is a founding advocate of Common Voices Coalition, a group that focuses on education regarding fire sprinklers and the role they play in a total fire-protection package for the home. Justina also serves in various capacities within the burn community. She has served as chat line moderator, support group leader, and panelist at the Phoenix Society World Burn Congresses. She is the current support group leader for the John S. Dunn Sr. Burn Center, as well as the burn unit team leader for Memorial Hermann Volunteer Services.

Printed in the USA
CPSIA information can be obtained
at www.ICGtesting.com
JSHW022328140824
68134JS00019B/1362